A Guide to Curriculum Planning in Health Education

Chet Bradley
Consultant
Health Education

Wisconsin Department of Public Instruction
Madison, Wisconsin

This publication is available from:

Publication Sales
Wisconsin Department of Public Instruction
Drawer 179
Milwaukee, WI 53293-0179
(800) 243-8782
www.dpi.state.wi.us/pubsales

Bulletin No. 6102

Printed on recycled paper.

Contents of the Guide

A Guide to Curriculum Planning in Health Education has been developed to provide tangible assistance and support to local school districts in the development of a comprehensive K-12 health instruction program. While this guide is not a mandated course of study, it is intended to assist you in planning a meaningful and relevant health education curriculum. The material presented here reflects the current thinking and experience of outstanding Wisconsin educators interested in and responsible for health education.

Consider these facts: (1) one million American workers call in sick each day, (2) more than 330 million work days are lost each year due to health-related causes, and (3) health care costs in this country exceed ten percent of the gross national product. In light of these facts, it becomes clear that our schools must make a major investment in the health education of our youth. I agree that, among state health policy issues, the most important are health education and health promotion in our schools. With nearly one million students in kindergarten through 12th grade in Wisconsin, and with 53,000 teachers and administrators available to work with them, this is surely the greatest opportunity we have to make a positive difference in the health habits of our young people.

This guide will provide a helpful framework for planning a comprehensive health instruction program, but the most critical component of a quality program is teachers who are interested, prepared, and committed to health education. With enthusiastic teachers who are working with the visible support of school board members, administrators, and parents, we really can lay the foundation for a healthier tomorrow.

Finally, school health education must not be taught in isolation. We must work to establish close relationships with health care institutions, community health agencies, and private businesses to help our schools become the centers for health promotion and health education in the 1990s.

John T. Benson
State Superintendent

Acknowledgments

The efforts of many individuals contributed to the development of this curriculum guide. The members of the State Superintendent's Task Force on Health Education deserve a special expression of appreciation. They devoted valuable time to preparing, critiquing, and revising drafts of the guide. The composition of the task force assured balanced input from representatives of elementary teachers, health teachers, administrators, and university health educators throughout Wisconsin. Task force members were

Chet Bradley
Health Education Supervisor
Wisconsin Department of Public Instruction
Chairperson and Content Editor

Nancy Blair
Curriculum Director
Kettle Moraine Public Schools

Robert Bowen
Professor–Health Education
University of Wisconsin–Stevens Point

Cathy Durkin
Elementary Teacher
Elkhorn, Area School District

Jon Hisgen
Health Education Teacher/Coordinator
Pewaukee Middle School
Pewaukee School District

Debbie Johnson
Health Education Teacher/Coordinator
Holmen High School
Holmen School District

Tom Kidd
Health Education Teacher/Coordinator
Osseo-Fairchild and Fall Creek School Districts

Chuck Regin
Assistant Professor–Health Education
University of Wisconsin–Whitewater

Diane Wedl
Elementary Teacher
Johnson Creek Elementary School
Johnson Creek School District

Joseph Wieser
Principal
New Holstein Elementary School
New Holstein School District

Carol Philipps
Nutrition Education and Training Coordinator
Wisconsin Department of Public Instruction
Ex Officio Member

Appreciation must also be expressed to the health education staff at the University of Wisconsin–LaCrosse for critiquing objectives for the ten content areas included in this guide.

As the task force developed this curriculum guide for Wisconsin schools, many resources from health education organizations, professional associations, and other state education agencies were reviewed. The following publications in particular provided many ideas and materials that were adapted or adopted for use in this guide.

A Guide to Curriculum Development for Health and Safety
State of Connecticut Board of Education – 1981

Essential Performance Objectives for Health Education
Michigan State Board of Education

Guidelines for Improving School Health Education K–12
Ohio Department of Education, Columbus – 1980

Health Education Curricular Progression Chart
National Center for Health Education
School Health Education Project

Health Education Framework
Department of Public Instruction
Olympia, Washington – 1980

Competency Goals and Performance Indicators K–12: Healthful Living
North Carolina Department of Public Instruction

Department of Public Instruction staff to be thanked are Telise Johnsen, text editor; Victoria Rettenmund and Jill Howman, graphic artists; Debra J. Motiff, word processor/typesetter; and Barbara Sebranek, program assistant.

Special thanks for cover photographs go to the Wisconsin Division of Tourism; additional photographs were provided by task force members and Neldine Nichols, DPI photographer.

Intended Use of This Guide

This curriculum guide was designed to be used by a local district health education curriculum committee or health education coordinating team responsible for the development, implementation, and evaluation of a K–12 health instruction program. It is *not* a teaching guide. However, teachers responsible for health instruction at any grade level should find the philosophy, goals, objectives, and other material provided in this publication useful as they plan their instructional programs.

In addition to being a resource for designing a K–12 curriculum, it is hoped that this guide will be used by teacher preparation institutions as a basic text in the preservice preparation of elementary education majors and also prospective secondary-level health teachers.

While this curriculum guide is not a mandated course of study, it does offer recommendations reflecting the current thinking of national, state, and local health education leaders. The State Superintendent's Task Force on Health Education believes that the components of this guide have the potential to be adapted or adopted at the local school district level in the design of a meaningful health instruction program.

Finally, this document must be considered a living curriculum which is always subject to change and continuous improvement. The Department of Public Instruction welcomes suggestions for improving the guide from those using it throughout Wisconsin.

Figure 1

The Comprehensive School Health Program

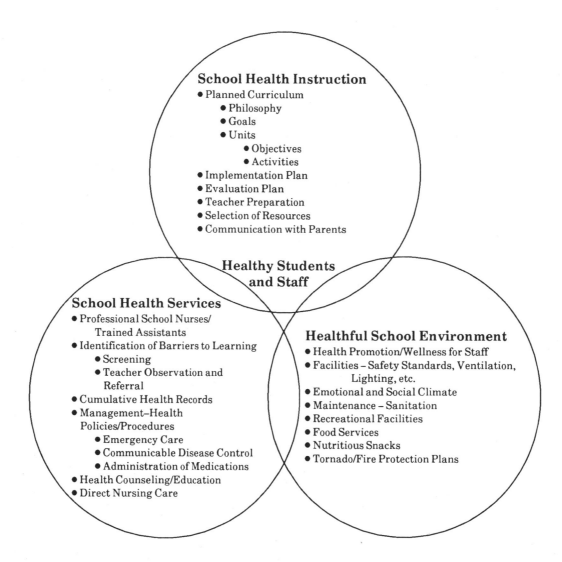

This diagram graphically illustrates the interrelation of health instruction, health services, and a healthful school environment, the three major components of a comprehensive school health program. The purpose of this publication, however, is to provide guidance for implementation of only one of these components—school health instruction.

Definitions

A definition is "the formal statement of meaning or significance of a word, phrase, etc." *(Random House Dictionary)* The following are the definitions adopted for key words and phrases used throughout this publication. Other publications may use variations of these definitions, depending on the authors' philosophical viewpoints and practical needs. Variation does not mean that one definition is necessarily more correct than another. It does mean that users of this publication need to be aware of how these words and phrases are being applied as they study this curriculum guide. The health education curriculum task force found the following definitions useful.

Health competencies are grade-level learner outcomes or expectations which include the knowledge, understandings, attitudes, and skills that are important for balanced intellectual, social, emotional, and physical growth and development.

A **health education curriculum guide** is a publication designed to provide ideas, directions, suggestions, and resources to persons planning, developing, or coordinating a health education program. It is not a teaching guide.

Integrated instruction is a coordinated effort to teach several different topics in several related disciplines. Health topics can and should be included as units of instruction in disciplines such as science, home economics, and social studies. Likewise, reading, writing, speaking, and computation skills can and should be strengthened within the health instruction program.

School health education is the development, delivery, and evaluation of planned learning activities which are developmental and sequential, kindergarten through grade 12, and are designed to positively influence the total health knowledge, attitudes, and behavior of individuals by increasing their abilities to make informed decisions.

The **school health education coordinating team** is composed of K–12 professional staff who have varied responsibilities related to health instruction within the school district. This team works under the direction of the school health education coordinator. Its members are representatives from each elementary, middle, junior high, and senior high school building. The team meets frequently to plan the continuous development, implementation, and evaluation of the district's health education program. In addition, each member serves as the instructional leader for health education within his or her school building.

The **school health education coordinator** is a person who provides the leadership and direction for planning, implementing, and evaluating a districtwide, comprehensive health education program required by State Statute 121.02 (1).

A **scope and sequence outline** details the major content areas taught and their sequential placement at various grade levels in the K–12 health education curriculum.

Time allocation refers to the minimum amount of time recommended in the curriculum guide for implementation of a comprehensive school health education program covering the ten major content areas.

Total health refers to the lifelong interdependence, constant interaction, and balance of the physical, emotional, social, and intellectual dimensions of human growth and development.

Overview

1

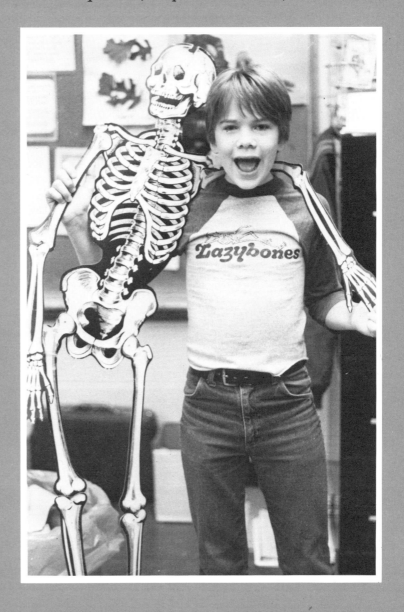

I

I'd rather see a sermon
>Than hear one any day;

I'd rather one should walk with me
>Than merely show the way.

The eye's a better pupil,
>And more willing than the ear;

Fine counsel is confusing,
>But example's always clear.

II

I soon can learn to do it,
>If you'll let me see it done;

I can see your hands in action,
>But your tongue too fast may run;

And the lectures you deliver
>May be very fine and true,

But I'd rather get my lesson
>By observing what you do.

For I may misunderstand you
>And the high advice you give,

But there's no misunderstanding
>How you act and how you live.

– Anonymous

Major public health problems such as suicide, accidents, venereal disease, heart disease, obesity, and alcohol and other drug abuse, along with health misconceptions, the lack of accurate health information, and the continuing rise in the cost of health care are but a few of the reasons for health education programs in schools.

Recognizing that many of these problems are preventable, practically all national and state health and education organizations have supported the development and implementation of comprehensive school health education programs. To cite some historical examples of additional support, *The National School Health Education Study* of 1963 states:

> It becomes increasingly evident that the possession of certain basic knowledge about health is essential if each individual ... is to achieve for himself, his family, and his community, an optimal level of health. Fundamental to this acquisition of such knowledge is a sound program of health instruction in the nation's schools ....

The study also revealed many problems related to school health education, including

> lack of coordination of health education programs throughout the school grades;
> inadequate professional preparation of staff;
> lack of interest on the part of some teachers assigned to health teaching.

Ten years later, in 1973, the president of the United States commissioned a national study of health education. *The Report of the President's Committee on Health Education* states that

> School health education in most primary and secondary grades is either not provided at all or is tacked onto other subject matter ... and is assigned to teachers whose main interests and qualifications lie elsewhere.

This study, just like the one that had been conducted 10 years earlier, made strong recommendations for the development and implementation of comprehensive school health education programs.

In 1974, the Wisconsin Governor's Health Policy Council, Committee on Health Education of the Public, conducted eight public meetings throughout the state to gain input from Wisconsin citizens concerning health education. The overwhelming testimony at these public hearings by the people of Wisconsin was that

Health education of children (K–12) is of the highest priority and aggressive efforts should be taken to insure adequate state financial support for implementation of statewide efforts in this arena.

In 1979, the surgeon general's report entitled *Healthy People* (followed in 1980 by a companion document entitled *Promoting Health/Preventing Disease: Objectives for the Nation*) outlined a national strategy for improving the health of Americans. Both publications reemphasized the critical need for quality school health education programs aimed at health promotion and the prevention of health problems.

In 1981, a national school health education task force created by the Education Commission of the States published a booklet entitled *Recommendations for School Health Education: A Handbook for State Policy Makers*. This document challenges state leaders in education, the health professions, and government to make a meaningful commitment to school health education.

In 1983, a study conducted by the Carnegie Foundation for the Advancement of Teaching published *A Report on Secondary Education in America* which recommended that a health education course be part of the required core curriculum in all high schools.

In June 1984, The Associated Press conducted an AP–Media general telephone poll which included a random scientific sampling of adults across the country. The approximately 1,200 participants were asked whether each of 13 common academic subjects should be graduation requirements for all high school students. Eighty-four percent of the respondents believed that health education should be a graduation requirement.

In addition to these examples, the following "quotable-quotes" from individual leaders and organizations at the national and state levels indicate broad–based support for the inclusion of comprehensive health education in the school curriculum.

Health education and promotion in our schools . . . is surely the largest opportunity we have to make a difference in the health habits of our citizenry.

Anthony S. Earl
Governor, State of Wisconsin

If communities establish partnerships among the schools, health care institutions, and private businesses, our schools have the potential to become centers for health promotion and health education in the '80s.

Herbert J. Grover
State Superintendent of Public Instruction
State of Wisconsin

The committee is unanimous in its firm belief that the only effective way [in] which the school can fulfill its responsibility for meeting health needs of youth is through comprehensive health education [in] grades K–12.

Joint Committee of the
National School Boards Association and the
American Association of School Administrators

It is a growing belief that any future advances made in improving the nation's health will not result from spectacular bio-medical breakthroughs. Rather, advances will result from personally initiated actions that are directly influenced by the individual's health-related attitudes, beliefs, and knowledge. School health education can make a valuable contribution in areas such as these and can play an important role in improving the quality of living.

American Medical Association

We believe that quality school health education programs designed to promote positive health lifestyles have the potential to prevent many of our health problems.

The State Medical Society of Wisconsin

Prevention is primarily an education program and belongs in the schools.

Vernon Wilson, M.D.
Vice President, School of Medicine
Vanderbilt University

No knowledge is more crucial than knowledge about health. Without it, no other life goal can be successfully achieved.

The Carnegie Foundation Report on
Secondary Education in America

However, even though school health education has received strong support from individuals and groups involved in both health and education, that support has taken the form of pronouncements rather than actions. *The time for action is now, and the implementation of well-planned health instruction in Wisconsin schools is long overdue.*

Philosophy

. . . health education can prevent health problems and improve the quality of life and total well-being.

When health care costs in the United States exceed 10 percent of the gross national product, the members of the State Superintendent's Task Force on Health Education believe it is time to implement meaningful health education programs in Wisconsin schools. These programs should be aimed at health promotion and the prevention of health problems. Task force members agree with health professionals and educators who believe that health education can prevent health problems and improve the quality of life and total well-being. As physician Ronald Vincent has stated,

> If our youth were given relevant information systematically and professionally, at a time in their lives when it could be of some value, they might very well solve the majority of these health problems themselves with that selfsame common sense that we do not give them credit for having. I propose to you, that if a solution to these medical problems does not come by the positive decisions of an enlightened youth, the solution is not likely to come at all.

Today throughout the country, the emphasis on health promotion and health education has never been greater. Schools in Wisconsin have the opportunity to make a positive impact on the lives of school-age youth. This is an opportunity they cannot afford to approach haphazardly in planning or halfheartedly in delivery.

Comprehensive health education develops skills for daily living and prepares individuals for their future roles as parents and citizens. Recent trends underscore the need for informed and educated individuals who have the knowledge, skills, and motivation to assume responsible roles in personal, family, and community health. Task force members believe that the commitment to comprehensive health education must be maintained now and into the next century. Educators and all citizens must guarantee that efforts are made to emphasize health as a value in life, and to enhance critical thinking, decision-making, and problem-solving skills regarding health. Quality health education motivates individuals to voluntarily take an active role in protecting, maintaining, and improving their health.

Quality health education motivates individuals to voluntarily take an active role in protecting, maintaining, and improving their health.

The overriding emphasis of this philosophy is upon having individuals successfully develop, establish, and achieve positive lifestyle goals. These goals enhance the probability of lifelong participation in health-promoting behaviors, with resulting total health benefits. Specifically, this philosophy is grounded in two fundamental principles. *The first is that health issues are approached in a positive manner.* Health education is a basic ingredient in a prevention formula. It can encourage the individual and the community to assume responsibility for the promotion of well-being and the prevention of disease and disability. Most premature deaths and

Health education is a basic ingredient in a prevention formula.

infirmities can be prevented by positive health practices and appropriate health care.

The second principle is based on the "whole person" concept, on recognizing that each individual is multidimensional. The physical, emotional, social, and intellectual dimensions of each person are dynamically intertwined and are influenced by time, setting, situation, and other people. Acknowledgment and nurturing of these interactions, both within the individual and between individuals, are critical to successful health promotion practices.

Most causes of premature death and infirmity can be prevented by positive health practices and appropriate health care.

Goals

This philosophy of positive health leads to and supports the following goals of a school health education program. Through health education, students will:

● know that total health includes all of a person's physical, emotional, intellectual, and social growth, development, and well-being;

● understand that every individual human being is valuable;

● appreciate that health is a right and a responsibility of every individual and community;

● realize that health professionals alone cannot solve health problems without individual and community support;

● understand that individuals can prevent most health problems through positive health behaviors;

● know that, to become partners in their own health care, individuals need accurate information, education, health–promoting services, and support;

● practice behaviors which promote and maintain intellectual, physical, emotional, and social well-being;

● contribute to family and community health and effectively use the health care system;

● practice principles of safe living and disease prevention to avoid health problems;

● appreciate the positive impacts that the individual, the family, and the community can have on environmental health;

● understand the structure and function of the human body and patterns of healthy growth and development.

Finally, a comprehensive health education program *can* make a difference and *can* influence the quality of life for this and subsequent generations. It is therefore with the greatest optimism and enthusiasm that improvement of the health status of our state's youth should be approached by the home/school/community team. The time for health education to emerge as a high priority in the curriculum has arrived. Positive health for all by the year 2000 is not only an attainable goal but an essential goal.

If one only considers the tremendous financial costs of preventable health problems, school health education and health promotion programs are economically irresistible.

Curriculum Framework

A basic task for any local district curriculum committee is to determine how the curriculum will be structured. There are many ways to organize the curriculum in health education, such as by unit, by concept, by competency, by domain, by problem, or by a combination of these.

This guide identifies ten major content areas as basic components of a comprehensive school health education program. They are taken from a 1981 report by a national health education task force and published in *Recommendations for School Health Education, A Handbook for State Policymakers*. These ten areas establish the overall framework for the body of knowledge to be included in a K–12 health education program. It is recommended that local districts develop their curricula around instructional units consisting of specific lessons which are developmental and sequential from kindergarten through 12th grade.

■ Figure 2

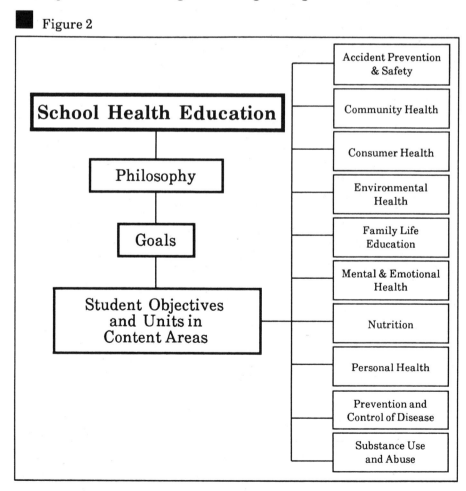

This guide makes specific recommendations for grade-level time allocation. These identify a minimum number of instructional periods needed at specific grade levels to cover the ten content areas in this guide. The primary purpose of making these recommendations is to attempt to describe a balanced approach to the K–12 health instruction program. In addition, the time recommendations are offered to suggest a realistic and practical way to implement health instruction as part of the total curriculum.

The time allocations at the K–6 level are especially important because the classroom teacher has the responsibility for providing health instruction along with all the other subjects required as part of the total elementary instructional program. At the junior and senior high school levels, the time recommendations are based upon a proposed discrete semester course meeting daily. *It is important to note that the recommended periods of instruction at the junior and senior high levels are based upon the assumption that the K–6 recommendations have been honored and meaningful instruction has occurred prior to the junior and senior high school years.* A primary concern here is that students understand the total health concept through developmental and sequential learning experiences at each appropriate grade level. Thus, if planned instruction does not begin until grade 4, the recommended times and objectives for grades K–3 must be given serious consideration.

While the amount of time allocated for health education at specific grade levels does not indicate the quality of that education, it is one criterion for determining the importance of health instruction in the total school program. The following chart gives time allocations in minimum number of instructional periods as recommended by the State Superintendent's Task Force on Health Education.

. . . the amount of time allocated for health education . . . is one criterion for determining the importance of health instruction in the total school program.

Recommended Time Allocation

	Recommended Time Allocation in Minimum Number of Instructional Periods to Cover the Content Areas at Specific Grade Levels*								
	Recommended number of periods per year One year = 34 Weeks							Recommended number of periods per semester	
	K	1-2		3-4		5-6		7-8-9	10-11-12
	45 min. per wk. 1 period = 15 min.	75 min. per wk. 1 period = 25 min.		100 min. per wk. 1 period = 25 min.		125 min. per wk. 1 period = 50 min.		1 course, meeting 90 periods in a semester. 1 period = 50 min.	1 course, meeting 90 periods in a semester. 1 period = 50 min.
School Health Education Major Content Areas for Classroom Instruction	Grade Levels								
	15-min. periods	25-min. periods				50-min. periods			
	K	1	2	3	4	5	6	7-8-9	10-11-12
I. Accident Prevention and Safety	15	12	12	15	15	6	5	5	14
II. Community Health	0	0	0	6	6	5	5	5	5
III. Consumer Health	0	0	0	6	6	5	5	10	8
IV. Environmental Health	0	0	0	6	6	5	5	10	10
V. Family Life Education	6	9	9	12	12	10	10	15	12
VI. Mental and Emotional Health	18	18	18	18	18	13	15	12	8
VII. Nutrition	18	18	18	18	18	10	10	5	5
VIII. Personal Health	18	18	18	18	18	13	12	10	9
IX. Prevention and Control of Disease	6	6	6	6	6	3	3	3	4
X. Substance Use and Abuse	6	9	9	15	15	15	15	10	10
TOTAL PERIODS	87	90	90	120	120	85	85	85	85

*The recommended periods for a year or semester *do not* necessarily mean that all instruction should be completed in that specific content area in consecutive lessons.

When one considers the task of institutionalizing a comprehensive health instruction program, one must realize that the process is continuous and never ending. There are three major phases involved in establishing a comprehensive program.

Development/Planning
Implementation
Evaluation

. . . the process is continuous and never ending.

The Department of Public Instruction has published a document entitled *A Continuous Path Toward a School Health Education Program: With Considerations for Achieving Success at Each Step.* This publication outlines for school districts eleven basic steps to follow in the development, implementation, and evaluation of a comprehensive school health education program.

The eleven steps are shown in figure 3. It is recommended that local committees planning a health education program seriously study *A Continuous Path Toward a School Health Education Program.*

A single copy of this document (Bulletin No. 0376) is available free; write or call the Department of Public Instruction, Publications Section.

The recommended philosophy, goals, objectives, and time allocations in this curriculum guide will be most useful to local school committees during Phase I: Development/Planning. Thus, the following discussion of Phase II: Implementation and Phase III: Evaluation is provided here for additional emphasis.

Figure 3

A Continuous Path toward a
School Health Education Program

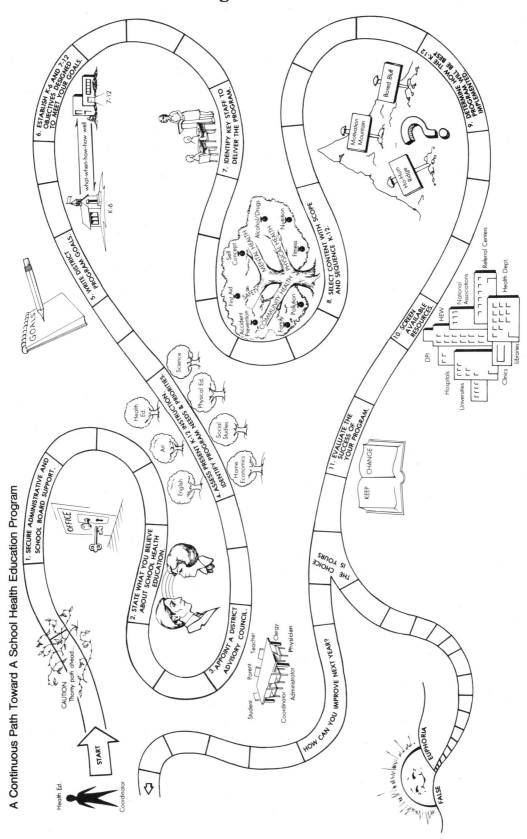

A Continuous Path Toward A School Health Education Program

Implementation

Once the curriculum components of a health instruction program have been developed, a realistic plan to implement the program in the classroom must be designed and set in motion. If at all possible, a district should plan on implementing the curriculum in two phases. Phase One would include the piloting of the new or revised curriculum. In order to test ideas, this short-range piloting phase may involve simply the use of activities and materials for a few weeks in classrooms during the developmental period. This limited range of activities may be most appropriate in small districts where only one or two teachers are involved in the curriculum change or where there are only one or two teachers per grade level. In other situations, the total curriculum may be piloted for a full year in one or more classrooms per grade level or course. Regardless of how limited or extensive the pilot phase, it has distinct advantages for a health education coordinating team gathering formative information before a total commitment is made to or significant changes are made in the curriculum. After pilot testing, the health education team usually makes changes in the proposed curriculum as a result of information obtained from students and teachers.

. . . a realistic plan to implement the program in the classroom must be designed and set in motion.

Phase Two is the long-range commitment to the implementation plan which outlines the process of transition from phase one to the diffusion of the program throughout the school district over several years. The coordinating team and administration must examine several critical issues prior to the complete diffusion of the new curriculum. The long-range implementation plan must address 1) staff responsibilities, 2) staff development needs, 3) implementation monitoring, and 4) the continuous modification of the instructional program. Each of these issues is dealt with separately in this section.

Identifying Staff Responsibilities

The successful implementation of any curriculum requires identification of key staff to pilot program components. The coordinating team should establish some specific criteria to be used in selecting staff during the pilot phase and also the long-term diffusion phase of the implementation process. All staff involved must clearly understand their responsibilities and the expectations related to the eventual implementation of the entire curriculum.

It is critical that the coordinating team and administration establish and implement a system of open, two-way communication and coordination among all staff involved. This requires a clear curriculum design so that everyone has a precise understanding of the rationale, philosophy, goals, objectives, content, scope and sequence, evaluation methods, and expected student outcomes for the total program. It is also extremely important that all staff involved develop a sense of legitimate ownership and commitment to the successful implementation of the curriculum.

It is . . . extremely important that all staff involved develop a sense of legitimate ownership and commitment to the successful implementation of the curriculum.

13

Identifying Staff Development Needs

Once staff have been identified and their responsibilities clearly articulated, staff development needs must be considered. Among questions to be addressed are the following.
- How does the new curriculum differ from the current curriculum?
- How will new learning experiences and teaching strategies be presented to teachers?
- How will background information needed to teach the content be provided to teachers?
- How will teachers be prepared to use any difficult materials?
- How will teachers learn to use the methods of evaluation?
- How will teacher ownership of the curriculum be nurtured?

A specific plan for professional staff development should be designed by the coordinating team and approved by the district administration. This plan should be based upon identified staff needs, considering
- a time commitment during the school year;
- budget;
- local teacher contract;
- who will lead and facilitate;
- who will attend;
- resources to be used; and
- immediate and long-range assessment of the value of the program.

Monitoring the Implementation Process

As the curriculum is implemented throughout a district, the coordinating team should set up some means of gathering observations from teachers, students, administrators, and parents. Formal monitoring to ensure that the curriculum is actually being implemented as designed is necessary during the implementation process. This monitoring provides for continuous formative evaluation of the program's success, both on its own merits and in terms of pupil achievements.

Formal monitoring to ensure that the curriculum is actually being implemented as designed is necessary . . . .

It is recommended that the building principal or a teacher with specifically assigned responsibility should serve as the instructional leader in the monitoring process. This person reports to the coordinating team the successes, failures, and changes necessary to keep the curriculum development, implementation, and evaluation processes continuous.

Modifying the Program

A final step in the long-range implementation of the curriculum is ensuring that improvements suggested by the results of formative evaluation will be implemented. At this point, the curriculum cycle begins to repeat itself, with continuing review and revision, reinforced by an appropriate professional staff development program.

Evaluation

One of the critical components of a comprehensive school health education program is the evaluation process. Evaluation begins with the initial planning of the curriculum and continues through the development and implementation of the instructional program.

In the curriculum development and planning stage, careful assessment of the existing program is necessary. Such a review serves both as an evaluation of present practice and an assessment of needs for change and development. In this stage, evaluation is a constant process by which the philosophy, goals, curriculum framework, scope and sequence, objectives, content, and learning activities are weighed against accepted educational philosophy and goals. During the implementation stage, evaluation consists of continuous monitoring of progress. Much of the evaluation will deal with student performance in terms of stated objectives. In addition, the district should evaluate areas such as availability of resources, teaching strategies, and classroom climate. Evaluation of such factors frequently provides insights into causes and possible solutions to educational problems.

The following are important considerations in the evaluation of a health education curriculum plan and the actual instructional program:

- agreeing on an evaluation plan;
- selecting appropriate evaluation instruments;
- establishing an evaluation schedule;
- implementing the evaluation plan;
- analyzing the results; and
- planning program modifications.

If both program goals and student objectives have been attained, no unusual curriculum revisions are indicated. When objectives have not been attained, the curriculum development cycle begins again.

In no instance should curriculum development stop completely. Even the best of programs can profit from continuous examination. New knowledge, improved techniques, changing philosophies, and local priorities make curriculum development, implementation, and evaluation a never-ending process.

Even the best of programs can profit from continuous examination.

Local school districts can use many different kinds of instruments for program evaluation. These include checklists, interviews, rating scales, structured discussions, surveys, and teacher-developed tests. Appendix D provides "A Checklist for Evaluating a School Health Education Program."

15

The following chart outlines key questions for teaching staff responsible for health instruction at any grade level. The completion of such an assessment can reveal much about the present status of health instruction, staff attitudes, and inservice needs.

SAMPLE SCHOOL HEALTH EDUCATION PROGRAM ASSESSMENT TOOL   GRADE LEVEL _____

PLANNED UNITS OF INSTRUCTION MAJOR CONTENT AREAS	How Well Is This Topic Covered	How Well Prepared to Teach Unit	How Important For Your Grade Level	Coordination and Communi- cation With Others/ Teaching Units	Major Emphasis of Instruction	Approximate Time Allocation No. Instruction Hrs. Per Year	Best Resources Used - People and/or Materials Briefly Identify	Resources Needed Briefly Identify
I. Accident Preven- tion and Safety	V S N	V S N	V S N	V S N	K A PS			
II. Community Health	V S N	V S N	V S N	V S N	K A PS			
III. Consumer Health	V S N	V S N	V S N	V S N	K A PS			
IV. Environmental Health	V S N	V S N	V S N	V S N	K A PS			
V. Family Life Education	V S N	V S N	V S N	V S N	K A PS			
VI. Mental and Emotional Health	V S N	V S N	V S N	V S N	K A PS			
VII. Nutrition	V S N	V S N	V S N	V S N	K A PS			
VIII. Personal Health	V S N	V S N	V S N	V S N	K A PS			
IX. Prevention and Control of Disease	V S N	V S N	V S N	V S N	K A PS			
X. Substance Use and Abuse	V S N	V S N	V S N	V S N	K A PS			

Key: V = Very   K = Knowledge
      S = Somewhat   A = Attitude Development
      N = Not at All   PS = Problem Solving

In addition to evaluating the total health education program, a district must also evaluate student performance in terms of program objectives. Teachers, administrators, and others will want to know how effectively students are developing health-related knowledge, attitudes, skills, and behaviors. Both objective and subjective evaluation procedures should be carried out. Some of these might be
- pre- and post-tests to determine student knowledge, attitudes, and skills related to health content covered;
- student self-evaluation scales, inventories, and surveys on health status and practices;
- simulations;
- interviews and discussions; and
- teacher and parent observations.

Assessing student performance in terms of knowledge gained is relatively simple. Constructing tests and other devices that allow students to demonstrate their knowledge about health is like constructing tests for any other curricular area. Testing should be both informal and formal, and should not be limited to paper and pencil situations. Activities that demonstrate use of knowledge should be included.

Evaluating student performance in terms of health skills is more difficult. However, the use of various simulations and problem-solving situations in which students must actually demonstrate their skills can be very helpful. Actual practice of skills learned will allow teachers to assess levels of student proficiency.

It is most difficult to assess attitudes and behaviors that promote lifelong health and well-being. However, attitude surveys, observations by teachers and parents of how students react in varying situations, and logs in which students record health behaviors and attitudes can be used to assess present performance. Long-term evaluation using follow-up surveys with both parents and students after students have graduated should also be considered.

In summary, the purpose of evaluation should be improving the quality of health instruction and of student learning experiences.

... the purpose of evaluation should be improving the quality of health instruction and of student learning experiences.

References

Boyer, Ernest L. *High School: A Report on Secondary Education in America.* The Carnegie Foundation for the Advancement of Teaching. New York: Harper & Row, 1983.

Healthy People: The Surgeon General's Report on Health Promotion and Disease Prevention. Washington, D.C.: U.S. Department of Health, Education and Welfare, Public Health Service, Office of the Assistant Secretary for Health and Surgeon General, July 1979.

Promoting Health/Preventing Disease: Objectives for the Nation. Washington, D.C.: U.S. Department of Health and Human Services, Public Health Service, Fall 1980.

Recommendations for School Health Education: A Handbook for State Policymakers. Denver, CO: Education Commission of the States, March 1981.

Report of Health Education of the Public Committee. Madison, WI: Governor's Health Policy Council, Wisconsin Department of Health and Social Services, 1974.

The Report of the President's Committee on Health Education. Washington, D.C.: U.S. Department of Health, Education and Welfare, 1973.

School Health Education Study: A Summary Report of a Nationwide Study of Health Instruction in the Public Schools. Washington,D.C.: 1964.

Vincent, Ronald G. "Physician's Role in the Health Program." *New York State Association Journal for Health, Physical Education and Recreation* (Spring 1970).

Preview of the Ten Major Content Areas

Arrangement
A Step Beyond: Creating Your Own Lessons
Interrelationship among Content–area Objectives

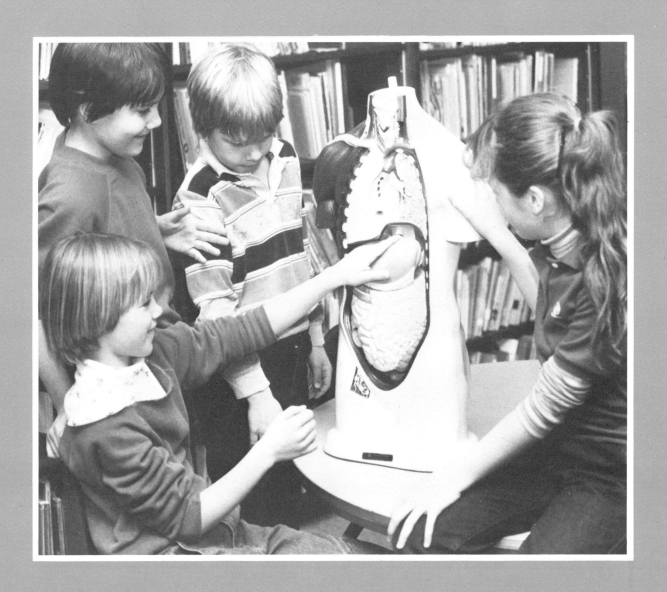

Arrangement

In this guide, the ten content areas are arranged in alphabetical order; each includes the following components.

Topics: examples of topics for which instructional units may be developed.

Rationale: brief background information concerning content–area problems, issues, and needs.

Life Goals: broad, individual lifestyle goals related to the specific content area.

Student Objectives: learner outcomes identified for each grade level, K–6, and for the junior high school and senior high school levels. These objectives are based upon minimum time allocations recommended for each content area at specific grade levels.

Sample Lessons: examples of learning activities in a format that can be implemented in the classroom to support specific student objectives identified in this guide. These lessons are included to illustrate how teacher creativity must be involved in implementing a quality health education program. Samples are provided in the ten major content areas for the primary, intermediate, junior high school, and senior high school levels.

These lessons are not intended to be complete in and of themselves. Each should be part of a complete unit of sequential instruction. Thus, it is assumed that students will come to each lesson with prerequisite knowledge and skills, and that subsequent lessons will provide review, expansion, and follow-up.

A Step Beyond: Creating Your Own Lessons

Delivering Content

This guide provides a comprehensive presentation of the philosophy, goals, and objectives which underlie a well-balanced health education curriculum. The guide is a primary resource for content information and suggests selected ways the content may be delivered.

For instruction to be most effective, it must interweave well-thought-out content with appropriately planned student activities and skillful teaching techniques. In summary, instruction occurs when the teacher:

- selects the content to be taught;
- assesses the students' prerequisite skills;
- makes appropriate adjustments in the level of difficulty of a content skill or the depth of a content concept;
- designs student activities directly related to the acquisition of the skill or concept;
- implements the lesson using valid principles of learning appropriately.

Designing a Lesson

For example, a selected objective might be: *The students will demonstrate the proper first aid treatment for a choking victim.* The teacher needs to examine this objective in light of what is known about the skill levels of the students.

Do students know the symptoms of a person who is choking? Can they distinguish between symptoms of choking and symptoms of other problems? Are students physically able, i.e., coordinated enough and large enough to administer the necessary type of first aid?

If the answers to the first two questions are *no* and the answer to the last question is *yes*, then the teacher may design a lesson that looks like this.

- On the board, generate two separate lists, one headed "Symptoms of a Choking Victim," the other headed "Symptoms That Might Be Confused with Choking."
- Compare the two lists to define the critical attributes that distinguish choking behavior from nonchoking behavior.
- Pass out slips of paper listing symptoms of people in different situations where choking might be the problem. Help students determine if the problem described is choking or something else.
- When satisfied that all students can identify a choking victim, discuss and demonstrate steps in the Heimlich Maneuver and the American Red Cross or American Heart Association procedures for treating a choking infant, child, or adult.
- Provide ample time and opportunity for students to practice and become proficient in this first aid procedure.

This particular lesson incorporates teacher input at the appropriate level of difficulty for the students, teacher modeling of correct behavior, checking for student understanding before going on to each new segment of instruction, and supervised practice to insure skill acquisition. In addition, a teacher would want to incorporate motivational techniques, opportunities to apply for review, and practice over time so that the skill be retained.

21

Using the Sample Lessons

The sample lessons in this document illustrate typical ways to effectively deliver the health education curriculum. Each is an attempt to show how to teach to an objective, incorporate sound instructional techniques, and use a wide variety of teaching approaches that may enhance student motivation and interest.

The lessons are only meant to be examples, however. Every teacher must make the critical decisions about student readiness for the material, integrate appropriate student activities, and develop complete units and lessons which reflect individual teaching style and creativity. This curriculum guide will be most effective when the teacher steps beyond the basic structure it outlines.

Interrelationships among Content-area Objectives

This curriculum guide is structured around the belief that the objectives presented in the content areas of Personal Health, Mental and Emotional Health, and Family Life Education can serve as the foundation on which a comprehensive school health education program can be built. The objectives in these three areas are essential to support the philosophy of health promotion/wellness and the prevention of health problems through positive health lifestyles presented in this guide.

It is important to review objectives in other closely related areas when adapting or selecting student objectives for any content area. Units organized in any content area should *not* be taught in isolation. The following outline lists content areas with close interrelationships.

Accident Prevention and Safety
Consumer health
Environmental health
Community health

Mental and Emotional Health
Personal health
Family life education

Community Health
Environmental health
Prevention and control
    of disease
Accident prevention
    and safety

Consumer Health
Nutrition
Prevention and control
    of disease
Substance use and abuse

Environmental Health
Community health
Accident prevention and
    safety
Prevention and control
    of disease

Family Life Education
Personal health
Mental and emotional
    health

Nutrition
Consumer health
Prevention and control
    of disease

Personal Health
Mental and emotional
    health
Family life education

**Prevention and Control
of Disease**
Community health
Environmental health
Consumer health
Nutrition

Substance Use and Abuse
Personal health
Mental and emotional health
Family life education
Consumer health

Accident Prevention and Safety

3

Focus
Student Objectives
Sample Lessons

Focus

Topics

Instructional units may be developed for these and other topics related to accident prevention and safety: attitudes toward safety, causes of accidents; home and school safety; traffic (auto, bicycle, school bus) safety; fire prevention; environmental hazards; poisoning prevention; first aid and emergency health care; cardiopulmonary resuscitation (CPR); safety personnel; resources and agencies; individual safety precautions; recreational safety; occupational safety; safety rules, laws, regulations, legislation, careers.

Rationale

. . . most accidents are preventable.

Accidents are the leading cause of disability and death among people from ages 1 to 24. Human and environmental factors can cause accidents, but most accidents *are* preventable.

Students, therefore, should develop a high degree of safety awareness. A continuous, sequential program covering safety, accident prevention, and emergency care, including CPR and first aid, can help students learn and practice safe ways to work, play, and live in our increasingly complex technological society.

Life Goals

The individual
- takes steps to correct hazardous conditions when possible;
- follows rules and procedures recommended for safe living;
- avoids taking unnecessary risks;
- applies correct emergency treatment when appropriate.

Student Objectives

See also Consumer Health, Environmental Health, Community Health

Kindergarten

Recommended Minimum Time Allocation: fifteen 15-minute periods/year

By the end of kindergarten, students will:

1. recite their names, addresses, and phone numbers;
2. explain what to do if they are lost;
3. recite the names of people who can help in case of an accident;
4. describe hazards at home, school, and on the playground and ways to avoid them;
5. identify poison signs that help people;
6. show in behavior and conversation that they recognize and appreciate the importance of having rules;
7. identify basic traffic signals and signs in the neighborhood;
8. explain and demonstrate how, when, and where streets should be crossed;
9. recognize that strangers, or even people they know, can be harmful.

Grade 1

Recommended Minimum Time Allocation: twelve 25-minute periods/year

By the end of first grade, students will
1. be able to dial the local emergency phone number in case of an accident;
2. list and recite necessary, basic information that should be communicated in an emergency;
3. identify and obey the safety rules at home, school, work, and play;
4. describe and demonstrate how to go to and from school safely;
5. describe and appreciate safety rules for bus and auto riding including the use of seat belts;
6. explain the correct fire drill procedure and behavior at home and at school;
7. describe basic steps to follow if injured at home or school;
8. discuss the importance of not eating or drinking unknown substances and name several common poisonous substances;
9. explain and demonstrate the use of warning stickers on hazardous household products;
10. talk about the dangers of getting into a car with a stranger.

Grade 2

Recommended Minimum Time Allocation: twelve 25-minute periods/year

By the end of second grade, students will
1. realize the dangers of playing with matches and fire;
2. discuss safety precautions around bodies of water, including ice;
3. describe and demonstrate the safe use of a bicycle;
4. identify and describe hazards which may result in injuries to the mouth, eyes, and ears;
5. discuss and demonstrate the safe use of electricity;
6. demonstrate basic first aid procedures for minor burns, wounds, abrasions, and animal and insect bites;

7. understand that individuals are responsible for their own personal safety;
8. design a fire escape plan with their parents for their homes;
9. state several reasons why it is unsafe to take dares;
10. identify ways to prevent accidents;
11. explain the proper steps to take in case of a tornado warning or other severe weather conditions.

Grade 3

Recommended Minimum Time Allocation: fifteen 25-minute periods/year

By the end of third grade, students will
1. discuss the dangers of "horseplay" in any situation;
2. discuss several important pedestrian safety precautions;
3. describe the benefits of wearing reflective clothing and using bicycle reflectors at night;
4. recognize, value, and respect safety personnel, like police officers and firefighters;
5. explain steps for home fire prevention and their home fire escape plans;
6. explain and appreciate the role of school safety patrols;
7. demonstrate respect for the laws and regulations regarding safety;
8. discuss hazards associated with lightning.

Grade 4

Recommended Minimum Time Allocation: fifteen 25-minute periods/year

By the end of fourth grade, students will
1. describe safety procedures for recreational activities such as flying kites, climbing, swimming, and hiking;
2. show concern for others' safety when in a group;
3. demonstrate safe bicycle behavior, rules of riding, and proper care of equipment;
4. develop a list of telephone numbers for emergency contacts;
5. recognize that minor injuries may require additional attention from responsible adults;
6. describe relationships between accidents and reckless, careless, and risk-taking behavior;
7. explain basic first-aid procedures for bleeding, resuscitation, poisoning, and burns.

Grade 5

Recommended Minimum Time Allocation: six 50-minute periods/year

By the end of fifth grade, students will

1. identify safe boating practices and water safety rules;
2. describe the correct procedure for helping someone who is in danger in the water;
3. explain the symptoms of and care needed by an infant, child, or adult who is choking.

Grade 6

Recommended Minimum Time Allocation: five 50-minute periods/year

By the end of sixth grade, students will
1. explain the symptoms of and basic first-aid procedures for treating unconsciousness, shock, and fractures;
2. list symptoms of major health problems such as heart attack and stroke and demonstrate the proper reporting procedures;
3. demonstrate a safe attitude toward risk-taking behavior and an understanding of its effect on themselves and others;
4. develop a babysitter's guide of accident prevention and safety procedures.

Grades 7-8-9, Junior High

Recommended Minimum Time Allocation: five 50-minute periods/ semester

By the end of ninth grade, students will
1. explain the proper first aid needed for an alcohol or drug overdose;
2. demonstrate mouth-to-mouth resuscitation on baby and adult manikins;
3. demonstrate the proper first-aid treatment for a choking victim.

Grades 10-11-12, Senior High

Recommended Minimum Time Allocation: fourteen 50-minute periods/ semester

By the end of 12th grade, students will
1. demonstrate application of dressings, bandages, and splints on an injured victim;
2. demonstrate the correct procedure of cardiopulmonary resuscitation on baby and adult manikins;
3. demonstrate responsible and safe behavior in high-risk situations such as driving, sports, and recreational activities;
4. know about a wide variety of career choices and occupational opportunities available in accident prevention and safety.

Grade 2 – Accident Prevention and Safety

Specific Topical Key: Fire Safety

Approximate Time: 50 minutes

Objectives

The students will design fire escape plans with their parents for their homes.
The students will be able to identify the procedures to follow in case of a fire in their house.

Activities

Draw a typical house outline, with all available exits, on the chalkboard.
Discuss
- all exits available in case of fire,
- all of the procedures to follow in case of a fire in their house (e.g., having a central meeting place in or outside the house, going to a neighbor's house, phoning fire department, using fire extinguishers, remembering special considerations for upper-level rooms, and so on).

Using the house outline on the chalkboard, develop a fire escape plan with your students.

Tell students to outline their houses with the help of their parents, and to develop their own fire escape plans. Ask them to discuss their fire escape plans with all family members, and bring copies of their plans back to school to earn fire safety certificates."

Resources Needed: Local fire department home fire escape checklist, fire safety certificate

Evaluation Focus
☒ Knowledge   ☐ Attitude   ☒ Problem Solving

Teacher's Notes (Things to change)

Grade 5 – Accident Prevention and Safety

Specific Topical Key: Choking

Approximate Time: 100 minutes

Objective

The students will explain the symptoms of and care needed by an infant, child, or adult who is choking.

Activities

Discuss the signs of choking and symptoms of a choking victim.

Discuss and demonstrate first-aid procedures to use with a choking baby or adult.

Pass out slips of paper listing symptoms of people in different situations where choking might be the problem. Ask students to determine if the problem described is choking, and if so, the proper procedures to use.

Ask students to explain the symptoms of choking victims and proper first-aid procedures to their parents, using a procedure checklist. Parents can assess student knowledge and sign the checklist, which students should being back to school.

Resources Needed: American Red Cross or American Heart Association manual, Heimlich maneuver filmstrip set, checklist

Evaluation Focus
☒ Knowledge ☐ Attitude ☒ Problem Solving

Teacher's Notes (Things to change)

Junior High – Accident Prevention and Safety

Specific Topical Key: Mouth to Mouth Resuscitation

Approximate Time: 200 minutes

Objective

The students will demonstrate mouth-to-mouth resuscitation on the baby and adult manikins.

Activities

Using manikins, teach students how to give effective mouth-to-mouth resuscitation to a baby and an adult.

Have students practice techniques on the manikins.

Ask students to explain the procedures to their parents or other family members, using a checklist which can be signed and brought back to school.

Resources Needed: American Red Cross filmstrip or film on mouth-to-mouth resuscitation, manikins, cleaning materials for manikins, checklist

Evaluation Focus
☒ Knowledge   ☐ Attitude   ☒ Problem Solving

Teacher's Notes (Things to change)

Senior High – Accident Prevention and Safety

Specific Topical Key: First Aid

Approximate Time: 50 minutes

Objective

The students will identify and/or demonstrate correct procedures in first-aid treatment.

Activities

This is a culminating activity covering all first-aid objectives and entitled: "First Aid Olympics."

At the end of the first-aid and emergency care unit, the instructor will develop a course with ten stations at which students will be required to perform cognitive or practical tasks to demonstrate their knowledge of first-aid procedures. Ten students will be chosen to run the stations, and award number scores based on accuracy to the participants.

The olympic contenders are to move from station to station and, within a time limit, answer questions or demonstrate the first-aid procedures required at each. Their scores are to be written on score cards. When all participants have completed all stations, their score cards are given to the instructor, who will compute point totals and determine first-through fifth-place winners. Ribbons or certificates can be given as awards.

Source: Jon Hisgen, School District of Pewaukee

Resources Needed: Materials for each station.

Evaluation Focus
☒ Knowledge   ☒ Attitude   ☒ Problem Solving

Teacher's Notes (Things to change)

Community Health **4**

Focus
Student Objectives
Sample Lessons

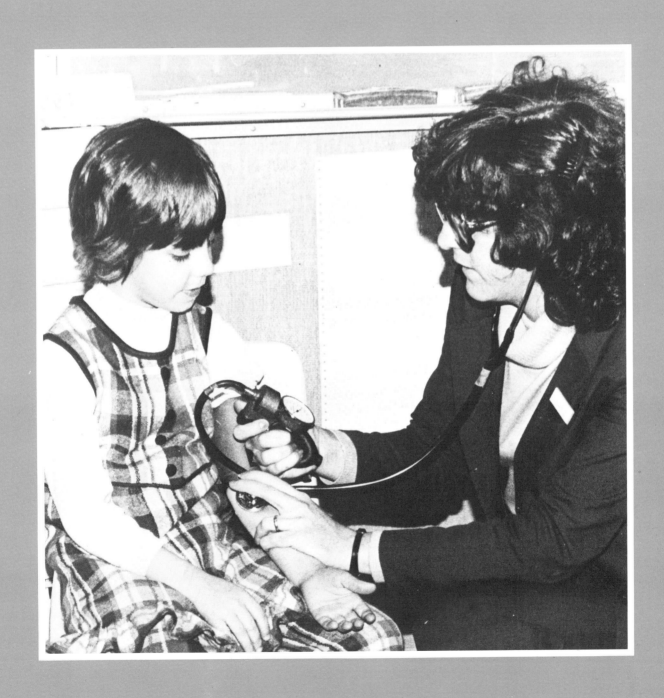

Topics

Instructional units may be developed for these and other topics related to community health: individual responsibility; healthful school, home, and community environments; community health resources and facilities; official and nonofficial health agencies; health service careers; pollution control; community involvement; current issues; trends in medical care.

Rationale

Whereas physical survival was the major public health concern in the past, psychological and social survival may well be the challenges of this age. Accordingly, community health efforts have begun to take into account the vast and complex network of sociological, psychological, and environmental factors that affect the health of people.

Schools have the potential ... to become centers of health promotion ....

Current trends in community health focus on individual responsibility and emphasize development of positive lifestyles and self-care skills which function cooperatively with established public health services. Individual responsibility for health is also a fundamental concept of all health education and supports personal and community efforts to promote optimal well-being for all citizens. Schools have the potential, in cooperation with community agencies and health care providers, to become centers of health promotion in the '80s.

Life Goals

The individual
● obeys laws and regulations designed to protect the health of the community;
● contributes to community health programs;
● accepts responsibility as a citizen for supporting the activities and programs of community health workers;
● avoids any personal action that might contribute to the deterioration of community health.

See also Environmental Health, Prevention and Control of Disease, Accident Prevention and Safety

Grade 3

Recommended Minimum Time Allocation: six 25-minute periods/year

By the end of third grade, students will
1. describe the characteristics of a healthy community;
2. cite examples of how people in the community work together to solve health problems;
3. identify ways to assist health agencies in the promotion of health.

Grade 4

Recommended Minimum Time Allocation: six 25-minute periods/year

By the end of fourth grade, students will
1. explain how community health agencies protect and promote the health and safety of community members;
2. list some human factors which influence community health;
3. identify roles of various public health workers;
4. know that health practices which contribute to personal well-being also support optimal community health;
5. know that disease prevention is a major role of public and private community health agencies.

Grade 5

Recommended Minimum Time Allocation: five 50-minute periods/year

By the end of fifth grade, students will
1. recognize the benefits that accrue when people in the community work together to promote health;
2. demonstrate awareness of the interrelationship between community health and well-being;
3. describe personal and family activities which influence community health;
4. discuss current community health issues;
5. list services various community health specialists provide.

Grade 6

Recommended Minimum Time Allocation: five 50-minute periods/year

By the end of sixth grade, students will
1. devise a plan by which an individual might work with others to promote a higher level of health in a community;
2. demonstrate how a group can implement a program focusing on a specific health issue within the school setting;
3. explain how the environmental health section of a health department serves the community;
4. explain the relationship of public health law to community health;
5. describe the major roles that volunteer health agencies and organizations play in promoting community health.

Grades 7-8-9, Junior High

Recommended Minimum Time Allocation: five 50-minute periods/ semester

By the end of ninth grade, students will
1. identify how a community can support and meet needs of different age groups;
2. identify local resources available to meet specific community health needs;
3. demonstrate knowledge of organizations and their positions on various health issues;
4. know about a wide variety of career choices and occupational opportunities available in community health.

Grades 10-11-12, Senior High

Recommended Minimum Time Allocation: five 50-minute periods/ semester

By the end of 12th grade, students will
1. demonstrate the skills needed to locate, evaluate, and use community health resources;
2. analyze the relationship between individual rights and the health of the community;
3. identify current trends in medical care;
4. implement a personal plan to actively investigate a current community health issue or support a community health campaign;
5. know that health education is an important function of community health agencies.

Grade 6 – Community Health

Specific Topical Key: Community Fitness Fun Run/Walk

Approximate Time: 50 minutes

Objective

The students will demonstrate how a group can implement a program focusing on a specific health issue within the school setting.

ACTIVITIES

As part of a school or community fitness day, students are to organize, publicize, and participate in a "Deck of Cards Run/Walk." Students, families, and friends may be invited to take part.

Set up a one-mile course on the school grounds, in the gymnasium, or in some other appropriate location. Use the following rules for the game.

Give each person who completes a one-mile run/walk five playing cards, chosen at random. Each must then decide if he or she has a "poker hand" worth keeping. If not, the participant may turn in all or part of the hand received and complete a second mile run/walk to earn replacement cards.

After each run/walk, a designated person must record each participant's name and the cards kept. Participants may run/ walk up to five miles to obtain the best possible "poker hand." When all have finished, the announcer names those with the winning hands. *All* participants should receive a certificate of merit for taking part in the run/walk.

Resources Needed: Many decks of cards, certificates of merit, announcer, person to serve as recorder

Evaluation Focus
☐ Knowledge   ☒ Attitude   ☒ Problem Solving

Teacher's Notes (Things to change)

Junior High – Community Health

Specific Topical Key: Appreciation of the Aging Population

Approximate Time: 50 minutes

Objective

The students will identify how the community can meet the needs of different age groups.

Activities

Each student interviews an individual 65 years of age or older. The interviewee can be a relative or a person known to the student, but preferably should be someone not known.

The following are suggested questions.
- What are the major problems that people your age face?
- What do you enjoy most about your life today?
- What services could the community provide to help meet your needs?
- If you could change one thing in your community, what would it be?
- What social activities would you like this community to provide?
- How do you think you can bring about the changes you desire?

Discuss responses to interviews and community action that might be taken to meet specific needs.

Resources Needed: Questionnaire

Evaluation Focus
☒ Knowledge   ☒ Attitude   ☐ Problem Solving

Teacher's Notes (Things to change)

Junior High – Community Health

Specific Topical Key: Wellness Newsletter

Approximate Time: (ongoing)

Objectives

The students will demonstrate the skills needed to locate, evaluate, and use community health resources.

The students will improve reading and writing skills while increasing their awareness of community health issues.

Activities

In this classroom activity, students are given a list of current "wellness" topics covered in such magazines as *Runner's World, Current Health, Family Health, Current Consumer and Life Studies,* and *American Health.* Each student will choose a topic of interest, locate a magazine with an article on that topic in the school library media center, read the article, and write a brief newspaper-style review.

Students may also choose to write personal-interest, personal-involvement, or local community-interest stories in lieu of magazine article reviews.

Student editors will choose acceptable articles on a range of wellness topics to be organized by content area in a newsletter. Student artists should be asked to provide appropriate art work throughout the newsletter. Arrange to have the newsletter printed or duplicated in some other way.

Copies of the newsletter can be distributed to students, at parent-teacher conferences, or at an open house.

Source: Jon Hisgen, School District of Pewaukee

Resources Needed: Current issues of health-related magazines or newspapers

Evaluation Focus
  ☒ Knowledge   ☐ Attitude   ☒ Problem Solving

Teacher's Notes (Things to change)

Consumer Health

5

Focus
Student Objectives
Sample Lessons

Focus

Topics

Instructional units may be developed for these and other topics related to consumer health: individual responsibility, influence of advertising, social and economic factors that affect health, laws for consumer protection (food labeling), protection agencies, health insurance, selection of medical services, quackery, reliable sources of health information, evaluating health products and services, use of trained medical personnel, criteria for product evaluation.

Rationale

Each individual is largely responsible for his or her own health. Carrying out this responsibility involves not only making critical choices in terms of one's lifestyle but also choosing among a vast array of medical and health-related services, products, and personnel. This combination of services, products, and personnel forms perhaps the fastest growing industry in the United States today, the health industry.

... the individual should be able to discriminate between what is valid and what is not.

Health-related information is widely disseminated via the media today, but the individual should be able to discriminate between what is valid and what is not. A person should be capable of identifying authorities on health, the various means of access into the health care system, and community public health resources. Students must acquire a certain level of sophistication in decision making by the time they reach adulthood.

Life Goals

The individual
- chooses health products and services on the basis of valid criteria;
- accepts only that health information provided by recognized health authorities;
- utilizes the services of qualified health advisors to help maintain and promote his or her own health.

Also see Nutrition, Prevention and Control of Disease, Substance Use and Abuse

Grade 3

Recommended Minimum Time Allocation: six 25-minute periods/year

By the end of third grade, students will
1. list commonly purchased health products;
2. identify the impact of advertising and other influences on the use of health products and services;
3. explain ways television advertising influences health product choices.

Grade 4

Recommended Minimum Time Allocation: six 25-minute periods/year

By the end of fourth grade, students will
1. identify questionable consumer health-related practices;
2. know that emotions, family practices, and values influence selection and use of health information, products, and services.

Grade 5

Recommended Minimum Time Allocation: five 50-minute periods/year

By the end of fifth grade, students will
1. explain how information on labels can be used in selecting health products;
2. explain why directions for use of over-the-counter and prescription health products must be understood;
3. differentiate between health quackery and legitimate health information and practices.

Grade 6

Recommended Minimum Time Allocation: five 50-minute periods/year

By the end of sixth grade, students will
1. identify media techniques used to advertize food, tobacco, alcohol, and health-related products;
2. evaluate accuracy of product claims;

3. examine reasons for selection and use of health-related products and services.

Grades 7-8-9, Junior High

Recommended Minimum Time Allocation: ten 50-minute periods/semester

By the end of ninth grade, students will
1. demonstrate the ability to think critically about health-related products and services;
2. analyze health-related products and services in terms of cost, quality, warranty, and availability;
3. demonstrate awareness of information, and the implications of information, on the use of prescription and over-the-counter health products;
4. identify criteria for the selection of appropriate health-related products or services;
5. demonstrate the ability to act upon concerns about ineffective health products or services.

Grades 10-11-12, Senior High

Recommended Minimum Time Allocation: eight 50-minute periods/ semester

By the end of 12th grade, students will
1. analyze techniques used to promote health-related products and services, including insurance;
2. describe consumer rights and responsibilities;
3. explain the functions and limitations of key governmental agencies regulating production, distribution, and promotion of health information, products, and services;
4. demonstrate the ability to apply valid criteria when selecting health-related products or services, such as fitness equipment, exercise programs, and alternative healing practices;
5. know about a wide variety of career choices and occupational opportunities available in the area of consumer health;
6. identify valid sources of information to refer to in making decisions about health services and products;
7. demonstrate an assertive attitude as a consumer wanting better health products and more responsible health services.

Grade 5 – Consumer Health

Specific Topical Key: Consumer Wellness

Approximate Time: 50 minutes

Objective

The students will differentiate between health quackery and legitimate health information and practices.

Activities

This activity can be used as an introduction to consumer health issues. Adopting the stereotypical "medicine man" approach, you are to try to "sell" your students on the virtues of Dr. Lemke's Stomachic Drops (perhaps even get some of them to say they will buy a bottle).

Hold up an old bottle filled with a fluid while you are talking. Explain that this bottle was found in an antique store and that Dr. Lemke's Stomachic Drops were actually sold in drug stores throughout the United States a number of years ago.

Use the following details in your presentation.
● I (the teacher) first got interested in the product as the result of a college assignment to recreate a medicine from a formula in an old medical text.

● I chose Dr. Lemke's formula because it was supposed to cure acne and split ends of the hair, common teenage complaints.

● The mysterious ingredient in Dr. Lemke's Drops is capsicum, which is grown hydroponically (submerged in water) and must be imported from Africa.

● My associates and I finished making the product in two months and successfully field tested it on ourselves and friends.

● We asked for support from the American Medical Association (AMA) and Bristol Myers, but were unsuccessful.

● We decided to market the product through magazines after receiving a patent, because the AMA and Bristol Myers would not give us their support.

● We bought a factory to grow capsicum and produce Dr. Lemke's Drops.

● We have increased sales each year for the last three years.

● A local newspaper is coming to take advertising pictures of students holding bottles of Dr. Lemke's Stomachic Drops.

● Famous people are endorsing the product, for example, the Osmonds and Michael Jackson.

● Students can get two bottles for the price of one if they bring their money the next time class meets.

47

When you have finished your presentation, and perhaps taken some orders for Dr. Lemke's Stomachic Drops from your students, stop the medicine man "pitch." Subsequent discussion should deal with the hoax that has been perpetrated, techniques you used to sell your product, and ways students can find reliable health information.

Source: Jon Hisgen, School District of Pewaukee

Resources Needed: Antique medicine bottle

Evaluation Focus
    ☒ Knowledge   ☒ Attitude   ☐ Problem Solving

Teacher's Notes (Things to change)

Specific Topical Key: Arthritis Quackery

Approximate Time: 50 minutes

Objective

The students will demonstrate the ability to respond to concerns about ineffective health products or services.

Activities

Three "To Tell the Truth" contestants are chosen at random one week before the game so they can study their responses.

An announcer and five panelists must also be chosen for this activity. To begin it, the announcer invites each contestant to stand and state name and occupation. Each does so, and then the announcer reads the introduction.

Script

Announcer: "Contestant #1 (#2, #3), state your name and occupation, please."

Contestant(s): "My name is Dr. Ernest (Edith) Callum. I am a physician specializing in the problems of the arthritic."

Announcer: "Dr. Callum has been a physician specializing in rheumatoid arthritis for the past 12 years. Dr. Callum's research deals with the environmental causes of arthritis and treatments that may relieve arthritic pain. Many of Dr. Callum's treatment techniques are patented and have been sold to over 200 hospitals throughout the world. Dr. Callum is a noted public speaker on the causes and cures of arthritis, and recently won the American Medical Association's Research Award for work on arthritis treatment. We will begin questioning with_____."

(panelist #1)

Each panelist gets two minutes to ask contestants questions from the list provided below.

Questions

1) What is arthritis?
2) Is there only one type of arthritis?
3) What causes arthritis?
4) How do you diagnose arthritis?
5) Who gets arthritis?
6) What form of treatment is most recommended?
7) What clinic or hospital do you work for?
8) Where did you earn your M.D. degree?
9) Are you affiliated with the Arthritis Foundation (AF) or the American Medical Association (AMA)?
10) What is the theory behind and how effective is the use of copper bracelets?
11) What is your opinion on arthritis-strength aspirin?
12) Would you prescribe orange juice and cod liver oil as a cure-all for arthritis?
13) What is liefcort?
14) Do vibrators help or harm the arthritic?
15) What is your opinion of treatment centers?
16) What are some of the steroid hormones used for arthritis treatments?
17) I understand only old people have arthritis. Is this true?
18) What are the symptoms of arthritis?
19) Is it all right to treat my arthritis myself?
20) Why does quackery thrive so much in our society?

After a break for a commercial that gives information on arthritis and/or quackery, each panelist votes for the contestant he/she thinks is the "real" Dr. Callum and tells the class his/her reasons for making this choice. The real Dr. Callum (contestant B) stands up at the end.

This activity can help prepare students to talk about quackery, health-related advertising, and sound bases for health decisions.

Source: Jon Hisgen, School District of Pewaukee

Resources Needed

Evaluation Focus
   ⊠ Knowledge   ⊠ Attitude   ⊠ Problem Solving

Teacher's Notes (Things to change)

Junior High – Consumer Health/Answer Sheet
Contestant A

1) Inflammation and pain in the joints.
2) Yes, the only kind is rheumatoid arthritis.
3) The major cause is cold, wet weather, but certain occupations such as typing can cause increased rates of arthritis.
4) With chemical screening techniques I have developed. These are used only at my clinic.
5) Only those who live where they are exposed to poor environmental conditions or who use their joints excessively.
6) The only successful approach is warm-oil treatments with constant electrical stimulation.
7) The Madison Clinic in California. It was named after my partner, James Madison.
8) Emporia Technical and Medical Institute in Emporia, California.
9) No; I don't believe in their philosophies.
10) If the metals are copper derivatives and are vibrated, they can, as has been shown at our clinic, have some curative effect.
11) I feel that all it is, is glorified aspirin.
12) I might for someone who has constipation but not for someone with arthritis.
13) I think it is the name of a type of arthritis of the hip.
14) The vibrator I have brought to the show has been used successfully in over 1,000 documented cases.
15) Since I run a clinic, I believe in their success and have thousands of testimonial letters to support my belief.
16) There are no hormone treatments used in my clinic. They can cause a loss of hair, you know.
17) Anyone can contract the dread disease of arthritis.
18) The only symptoms are pain and a tingling sensation at the arthritic joint.
19) If one has secured the proper devices and attended my clinic for three weeks then one can self-treat.
20) Because there are unqualified people looking for a quick buck, and there are millions of gullible Americans looking for a quick cure.

Junior High – Consumer Health/Answer Sheet
Contestant B

1) A rheumatic disease. An inflammation of the joints.
2) No, there are several kinds. The most common type is rheumatoid arthritis.
3) Scientists are not sure. Causes are being studied. Some feel that it is caused by bacteria or a virus.
4) I use x-rays and a careful evaluation of each patient's symptoms.
5) Anyone can contract arthritis.
6) Treatment by a physician, rest, freedom from mental strain, a balanced diet, and aspirin.
7) The Madison Clinic in Sacramento, California.
8) Marquette University in Milwaukee, Wisconsin.
9) Yes, I have been for 12 years, ever since I started practicing medicine.
10) Many metals are said to have curative powers. I do not know the theory.
11) They are selling this "glorified aspirin" through high-pressure advertising. The only active ingredient in the product is the aspirin.
12) I do not feel promoters of these remedies are reliable sources of health information.
13) A drug claimed to cure arthritis concocted by Dr. Robert Liefman.
14) They might relieve the pain, but they will not cure arthritis. In addition, when rest of a joint is essential, they could be harmful.
15) I feel these treatments are totally ineffective.
16) ACTH (Cortropin) Cortisone.
17) No, it can affect the young as well.
18) a) Persistent pain or stiffness, b) pain or tenderness in one or more joints, c) swelling in one or more joints, d) recurrent symptoms when they involve more than one joint, e) tingling sensation in the fingertips, f) fever, weakness.
19) No, because self-treatment could be harmful and aggravate the condition.
20) Because people are looking for the ultimate cure. They will go to any lengths to relieve pain.

Junior High – Consumer Health/Answer Sheet
Contestant C

1) An inflammation and corresponding pain in the joints.
2) No, there are thousands of kinds of arthritis, but they can all be cured in the same way.
3) The major cause is the type of food we eat. High acid content can lead to arthritic joints.
4) By looking for lumps over or under the joints.
5) Only those who abuse their bodies with poor diet.
6) A special high-oil, low-protein diet is the only successful treatment.
7) The Madison Arthritis Clinic in Sacramento, California.
9) No, the costs of membership far outweigh the benefits.
10) Only if the copper is taken internally will it have a beneficial effect.
11) I concur with the other contestants; the only active ingredient is aspirin.
12) I have had great success with this same treatment at my clinic. I take offense at anyone calling it unreliable or a cure for constipation.
13) I am sorry, but I don't know.
14) The vibrating machine I have brought here today has been sold to over one million arthritic patients. It should be used in conjunction with my diet therapy for best results.
15) I believe that they can be successful only if they are run by sound medical people and qualified nutritionists, like those my treatment center happens to have.
16) The only hormone I use is a new patented one called Callumisone developed and administered exclusively by me.
17) Yes, only old people tend to develop arthritis, as their nutritional problems have continued over a long period of time.
18) The only symptoms are pain and a distinctive swelling above and below the joints.
19) After a stay at my clinic, any person should have the nutritional knowledge to overcome the pain, the discomfort, and the disease itself.
20) Because our government does not punish quacks enough.

Senior High – Consumer Health

Specific Topical Key: Health Club Survey

Approximate Time: 50 minutes

Objective

The students will apply valid criteria in the selection of health-related products or services, including fitness equipment, exercise programs, and alternative healing practices.

Activities

Give your students the accompanying survey to fill out. As they complete it, they will become aware of what they feel are the important features of a worthwhile health club or exercise facility. It may be helpful to translate possible ratings, or discuss them, before students begin. *High importance* might translate as *essential*, *medium* as *good*, but not *essential*, and *low* as *marginal* or *irrelevant*, for example.

Evaluation Focus
    ⊠ Knowledge   ⊠ Attitude   ⊠ Problem Solving

Teacher's Notes (Things to change)

Senior High – Consumer Health

Survey Directions

What do you feel are the important features of a worthwhile health club or exercise facility? Indicate the importance of the item(s) mentioned in each question below by circling one of the three numbers.

		Importance	
Facility	**High**	**Medium**	**Low**
1. Does the club have an indoor jogging track?	2	1	0
2. Is there a swimming pool?	2	1	0
3. Are the men's and women's locker rooms equal in size?	2	1	0
4. Does the club have a Universal weight machine?	2	1	0
5. Does the club have a carpeted or matted exercise area?	2	1	0
6. Is there a lounge or rest area?	2	1	0
7. Are there racquetball courts?	2	1	0
8. Is there a whirlpool and sauna available to both men and women?	2	1	0
9. Are there indoor tennis courts?	2	1	0
10. Is there reserved parking for members?	2	1	0
11. Is the club within walking distance from home or work?	2	1	0
12. Does the club have a play area for children?	2	1	0
13. Is there a lab available for testing health and fitness levels?	2	1	0
14. Are there eating facilities?	2	1	0
15. Does the club provide personal items such as soap, towels, shampoo, and so forth?	2	1	0
16. Is rental equipment available?	2	1	0

Program and Personnel

	High	**Medium**	**Low**
17. Is the staff well trained and qualified?	2	1	0
18. Are all instructors trained in the areas of first aid, for example, CPR, artificial respiration, water safety?	2	1	0
19. Are lessons offered for sports activities?	2	1	0
20. Is there an introductory offer for prospective members?	2	1	0
21. Is there a good variety of organized classes?	2	1	0
22. Is there a weight reduction program?	2	1	0
23. Is the staff friendly and eager to help?	2	1	0
24. Is the staffing ratio per member adequate?	2	1	0
25. Does the club sponsor any competitive teams?	2	1	0

Costs and Membership	High	Medium	Low
	Importance		
26. Are the services of a masseuse available?	2	1	0
27. Does the club send out flyers to inform members of new programs, classes, tournaments, and so forth?	2	1	0
28. Is there adequate security for personal belongings?	2	1	0
29. Are there children or family memberships available?	2	1	0
30. If a family membership is available, is there a reduction in cost?	2	1	0
31. Are all programs and facilities included in the membership cost?	2	1	0
32. Is the yearly cost $100 or less?	2	1	0
33. Are you allowed to bring a guest?	2	1	0
34. Is the duration of the membership a year, or can you join on a monthly or half year basis?	2	1	0
35. Are partial memberships available for certain sessions, classes, or sports?	2	1	0
36. Are you bound by a legal contract when joining?	2	1	0
37. Is the club adequately insured for liability and injury?	2	1	0
38. Is there a refund if the club is closed?	2	1	0
39. Is your membership honored by other clubs of the same organization?	2	1	0
40. Is there a senior citizens discount?	2	1	0

Rating

The purpose of this survey is to find out what you as a consumer feel are the features a good health club should have. Therefore, you should be interested primarily in the number of 2s in your responses. Count them. The categories below will tell you whether you are likely to find a health club that meets your requirements.

30-40. What you are looking for is a club which provides a more than adequate program and facility. Unfortunately, one that has these exceptional features is rarely to be found. If you do find one that offers everything you require, it may be too expensive for an individual to join.

20-29. You are looking for an average health club. These exist in good numbers; usually their membership and other fees are reasonable. Remember, though, that individuals have preferences in programs and facilities. You might have to visit a number of health clubs to find the one that has most of the programs you feel are important.

0-19. First, determine whether or not you are at all interested in any type of health club. If you are, re-evaluate what you feel are the important features of such a club. It may be that you are the type of individual who can carry out a balanced fitness program or participate in sports without the aid of an organized club.

To complete the activity, discuss with students their reasons for rating some items in the survey "1" or "0."

Environmental Health 6

Focus
Student Objectives
Sample Lessons

Topics

Instructional units may be developed for these and other topics related to environmental health: individual and community responsibility, pollution, effects of environment on health, environmental protection agencies, population density, world health, waste disposal, sanitation, laws, career choices.

Rationale

The protection of health and the promotion of human comfort and well-being through interactions with the environment are responsibilities which result from modern conditions. The increase in population and diversity of human activities have made control of their impact on the environment increasingly difficult.

Large-scale programs of sanitation and environmental protection have attempted to resolve the various problems of pollution. *The critical factor affecting success of such programs is neither their scope nor their funding, but the degree to which each individual values the environment and cooperates in cleaning and protecting it.*

. . . the student must become actively involved in promoting improvement of the environment.

In order to become a responsible citizen, the student must first recognize what constitutes the environment and the resources that exist to protect and improve that environment. Secondly, the student must become actively involved in promoting improvement of the environment.

Life Goals

The individual
- obeys laws and regulations essential for the survival of humanity;
- understands that all people have a responsibility to help conserve resources;
- avoids actions that contribute to the deterioration of the environment;
- utilizes agencies responsible for environmental protection.

Also see Community Health, Accident Prevention and Safety, Prevention and Control of Disease. Special note: See A Guide to Curriculum Planning in Environmental Education.

Grade 3

Recommended Minimum Time Allocation: six 25-minute periods/year

By the end of third grade, students will
1. list ways people can help keep a healthy environment;
2. participate in a program aimed at reducing litter in school and community;
3. know and demonstrate ways individuals and groups can help keep the school environment healthy;
4. describe ways the senses can be protected from air pollution;
5. differentiate between kinds and sources of environmental pollution.

Grade 4

Recommended Minimum Time Allocation: six 25-minute periods/year

By the end of fourth grade, students will
1. identify and discuss individual and community responsibilities for the prevention and control of environmental problems;
2. describe community facilities and procedures that ensure safe water supplies and sanitary trash and sewage disposal;
3. demonstrate ways water can be conserved at home and elsewhere;
4. discuss reasons why humans need natural parks and recreational sites;
5. list health problems associated with water pollution;
6. describe the impact water pollution has on well-being.

Grade 5

Recommended Minimum Time Allocation: five 50-minute periods/year

By the end of fifth grade, students will
1. describe methods used to prevent or curtail land pollution practices;
2. list the sources of and methods for dealing with solid waste;
3. demonstrate an appreciation of the beauty and importance of natural resources and of their impacts on human health;
4. explain the relationship between population and land use;

5. predict environmental changes that will be caused by increasing populations;
6. describe the impact of land pollution on well-being.

Grade 6

Recommended Minimum Time Allocation: five 50-minute periods/year

By the end of sixth grade, students will
1. describe ways in which improving the environment can enhance physical, mental, and social health;
2. list negative and positive environmental changes that may have come about by the year 2000;
3. explain why sanitation is important to the nation's health;
4. explain the effects of environmental practices on well-being;
5. describe how rodent and insect populations can be affected by environmental practices.

Grades 7-8-9, Junior High

Recommended Minimum Time Allocation: ten 50-minute periods/semester

By the end of ninth grade, students will
1. describe the impact technology has on the environment and human health;
2. identify local, state, and federal agencies that promote or affect environmental health;
3. discuss the individual's responsibility for preserving a healthy environment;
4. compare the origins and impact on well-being of various types of air, water, and land pollution;
5. describe the effects of noise pollution on well-being;
6. list potential environmental carcinogens;
7. discuss sources of radiation;
8. know that over the past 100 years environmental control measures have greatly reduced human illness.

Grades 10-11-12, Senior High

Recommended Minimum Time Allocation: ten 50-minute periods/semester

By the end of twelfth grade, students will
1. predict what the environment will be like in 50 years if people continue to make positive environmental changes;
2. analyze the roles of agencies that address environmental issues;
3. demonstrate ways of preserving a healthy environment in the school and community;
4. analyze the pros and cons of various types of energy;
5. evaluate the environmental impact of toxic waste burial;

6. know about a wide variety of career choices and occupational opportunities available in the environmental health field;

7. discuss improvements in air and water quality which have been made through public and private control measures;

8. talk about how individual and societal values affect decisions policy makers and citizens make about environmental health;

9. describe how personal and family lifestyles affect the environment;

10. recognize that government regulation of environmental quality is not fully accepted by various groups in this society.

Grade 3 – Environmental Health

Specific Topical Key: Reducing Litter

Approximate Time: 25 minutes

Objective

The students will participate in a program aimed at reducing litter in school and community.

Activities

"Caught in the Act of Cleaning the School" is the name of this activity. During a given week, all third-grade students are designated official "watchdogs" (cleanup collies) to keep an eye out for any person in the school who can be caught in the act of improving the school environment by picking up litter, straightening hall areas, and so on.

When a watchdog spots a student doing a good deed, he or she returns to the classroom and files a report with the teacher, indicating both who did the clean deed and exactly what was done. The watchdog is then given permission to fill out an official award certificate to present to the student in the homeroom. The student's name and deed are also posted on a school bulletin board of "Most Appreciated School Citizens."

Resources Needed: Certificates

Evaluation Focus

☐ Knowledge   ☒ Attitude   ☒ Problem Solving

Teacher's Notes (Things to change)

Junior High – Environmental Health

Specific Topical Key: Noise Pollution

Approximate Time: 50 minutes

Objective

Students will describe the effects of noise pollution on well-being.

Activities

Students conduct a noise pollution survey of their own environment using a decibel meter.

Working in groups, students measure noise levels in a variety of locations such as the classroom, a gymnasium during athletic events, the lunch room, and shops; they also measure noise from sources of music. Students record results in chart form, listing the source of each sound, the area where it was recorded, and its decibel level.

Students rank sounds according to their decibel levels and determine whether each sound could be detrimental to their health. They can discuss ways to minimize the hazards of noise pollution.

Resources Needed: Decibel meter

Evaluation Focus
☒ Knowledge   ☐ Attitude   ☒ Problem Solving

Teacher's Notes (Things to change)

Senior High – Environmental Health

Specific Topical Key: Toxic Waste

Approximate Time: 50 minutes

Objective

Students will evaluate the environmental impact of toxic waste burial.

Activities

The students are to become part of a mock public hearing that will study the effects of waste disposal, water poisoning, soil contamination, and possible health hazards.

Before the date of the activity, each student should have the opportunity to observe and discuss each of the following topics: solid land fill sites, industrial water pollution, and the effects of chemical burial sites. Each student should have read about and discussed Love Canal (Niagara, NY). In addition, the students are to have read selected environmental protection agency reports on ground water problems.

The students will form small groups of six or seven.

Each group will conduct its own public hearing on whether or not the dumping of wastes should be allowed to continue at the site pictured below.

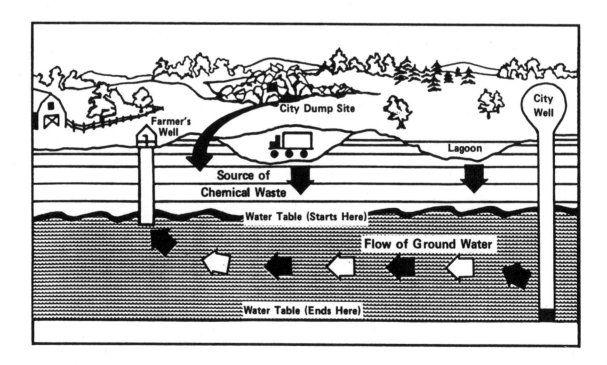

Each person in the group will assume one of the roles listed below:

● farmer;

● trash collector who dumps the trash, lives in the city, and consumes city water;

● president of the company who is dumping chemical wastes;

● conservationist who once used the land for hunting and fishing;

● a city dweller who receives water from the city well;

● an official from the neighboring community where the next dumping might be if this site is closed;

● the judge who will make the final decision to either grant the license to continue to dump or rescind the license.

Source: Jon Hisgen, School District of Pewaukee

Resources Needed: Diagram of dumping site and potential impact on a community

Evaluation Focus

    ☒ Knowledge   ☐ Attitude   ☒ Problem Solving

Teacher's Notes (Things to change)

Family Life Education

7

Focus
Student Objectives
Sample Lessons

Focus

Topics

Instructional units may be developed for these and other topics related to family life education: family composition and roles, life cycles, human growth and development, the reproductive process, heredity, marriage, selecting a compatible life partner, family relationships, improving family communications, parenting, prevention of abuse.

Rationale

Family living is characterized by dynamic personal and group experiences which can be enhanced by developmental support from many sources. The family is the major forum for developmental experiences; however, the school does offer significant resources for guiding young people toward positive personal adjustment, preparation for marriage, and family living. Societal problems and challenges associated with issues such as teenage pregnancy, divorce, and single-parent families can be confronted through effective school-based instruction in family living.

In identifying its role, the school recognizes the primacy of parental responsibilities for the basic education of their children for family living. The school supports both parents and children in their efforts to gain the knowledge and learn the behaviors that enhance the family foundation of society.

There are a number of family problems, such as child abuse and neglect, which are intensified by economic distress, social distance within communities, personal and family dynamics, and the breakdown or lack of community and family support. Successful education involving students, teachers, parents, and other community resources can help prevent many of them.

The school supports both parents and children in their efforts to gain the knowledge and learn the behaviors that enhance the family foundation of society.

Life Goals

The individual
- respects the rights and privileges of every family member;
- adjusts appropriately to changing physical, mental, emotional, and social roles, responsibilities, and privileges as they occur throughout the life cycle;
- deals comfortably and appropriately with the demands of his or her own gender;
- communicates effectively as a member of a family and of society;
- supports the belief that the health of all children is an individual, family, and community responsibility.

See also Personal Health and Mental and Emotional Health.
   Special note: See "Instruction about Human Sexuality" in section 13 on "Current and Future Issues in School Health Education."

Kindergarten

Recommended Minimum Time Allocation: six 15-minute periods/year

By the end of kindergarten, students will
1. respect and be courteous about similarities and differences in human beings;
2. describe qualities of friends;
3. describe what parents and children do to promote a healthy family;
4. discuss ways that strangers or even people they know can be harmful;
5. understand that every child has the right to accept or reject affection.

Grade 1

Recommended Minimum Time Allocation: nine 25-minute periods/year

By the end of first grade, students will
1. describe the groups they belong to and how to work cooperatively in any group;
2. describe various kinds of families and the ways family membership can change;
3. discuss individual and group responsibilities in a family and ways the family works together as a unit;
4. realize that, if approached by a stranger with a gift, a promise, a ride, or a threat, they should say "no," and run to tell someone they trust;
5. name animals that reproduce their own kind;
6. realize both animals and humans have mothers and fathers who care for their young.

Grade 2

Recommended Minimum Time Allocation: twelve 25-minute periods/year

By the end of second grade, students will
1. cite examples of ways specific individuals of the same age are similar and different in their growth;
2. realize that if children are loved and their physical needs met, they feel safe and secure;
3. recognize and value caring adults who are significant in their lives;

4. name a variety of fun activities family members participate in to-gether to show caring for one another;
5. recognize that human beings grow and develop inside their mothers;
6. realize that human beings can be abused physically, socially, and emotionally in different ways and by different people.

Grade 3

Recommended Minimum Time Allocation: twelve 25-minute periods/year

By the end of third grade, students will
1. explain why children need families and how family members contri-bute to the physical and mental health of one another;
2. describe different kinds of friendships;
3. identify different stages of the life cycle from birth to death;
4. explain the contributions, responsibilities, rights, and privileges of each family member;
5. illustrate ways family members and significant others help and influ-ence attitudes and behavior;
6. identify trusted people who can help with personal and family difficul-ties;
7. identify the different ways living things reproduce.

Grade 4

Recommended Minimum Time Allocation: twelve 25-minute periods/year

By the end of fourth grade, students will
1. use accurate terminology to explain the structure and function of the human reproductive system;
2. identify the changes which occur as they approach puberty;
3. realize that learning to get along with others is a unique process for each individual;
4. describe how they are affected by and affect those with whom they associate;
5. illustrate relationships in a family that influence the health, happi-ness, and harmony of the family unit;
6. realize that each person's family is unique and special;
7. define different types of personal abuse and know where to get help if abuse occurs.

Grade 5

Recommended Minimum Time Allocation: ten 50-minute periods/year

By the end of fifth grade, students will
1. explain the structure and function of the human reproductive system;

2. explain physical, emotional, and social changes which occur as they approach puberty;
3. list the characteristics that help maintain friendships and compare their own characteristics with those on this list;
4. appreciate the impact of the family on, and importance of the family to, individual development;
5. identify the possible impacts of death or divorce on the family;
6. realize that the roles of each member of the family may change for a variety of reasons.
7. analyze the difference between assertiveness and aggression.

Grade 6

Recommended Minimum Time Allocation: ten 50-minute periods/year

By the end of sixth grade, students will
1. analyze the impact of peer pressure on an individual and a group;
2. describe specific roles of parents and children that are complimentary and/or conflicting;
3. appreciate that a positive family environment will encourage communication among members;
4. demonstrate an understanding that values and attitudes about family life come from the family unit;
5. explain basic steps involved in making a rational decision;
6. discuss dating as one way of exploring friendships and learning new social skills;
7. identify criteria for acceptable dating behavior.

Grades 7-8-9, Junior High

Recommended Minimum Time Allocation: fifteen 50-minute periods/ semester

By the end of ninth grade, students will
1. investigate interrelationships of and disparities among physical, emotional, and social changes occurring at puberty;
2. understand a pregnant mother's ability to affect healthy embryonic and fetal development;
3. identify the sequence of events which show, in general, the development of the human organism from conception through adulthood;
4. develop the ability to resolve conflicts and formulate new friendships;
5. accept and value human sexuality as normal and essential to total well-being;
6. identify factors that influence their sexual attitudes;
7. recognize the value and necessity of facilitating communication about sexuality with parents;
8. identify the responsibilities and consequences inherent in sexual relationships;

71

9. identify the general reasons for and methods of preventing pregnancy;
10. discuss the physical, emotional, and social problems associated with teenage pregnancy;
11. develop, using a decision-making process, a code of behavior for themselves that is consistent with a positive value system and positive goals;
12. know that the need for love and affection influences behavior.

Grades 10-11-12, Senior High

Recommended Minimum Time Allocation: twelve 50-minute periods/ semester

By the end of 12th grade, students will
1. identify the major causes of birth defects such as rubella, drugs, heredity, and communicable diseases;
2. understand factors that promote healthy embryonic and fetal development, and especially the effects of nutrition;
3. explain that it is possible to plan for or to avoid pregnancy, and that the decision is influenced by many factors;
4. recognize problems associated with teenage pregnancy which affect the teenager, friends, family, and community;
5. know facts about sexual assault and its prevention;
6. recognize and appreciate their values and goals and how these relate to selection of a spouse;
7. describe factors which contribute to a successful marriage and family unit;
8. analyze the impact of children on a family, including role changes, responsibilities, and costs;
9. analyze the interrelationships among career and family roles, various responsibilities, and family harmony;
10. know about a variety of career choices and occupational opportunities available in the area of family life and health.

Grade 1 – Family Life Education

Specific Topical Key: Kinds of Families

Approximate Time: 50 minutes

Objective

The students will describe the various kinds of families and the ways family membership can change.

Activities

Present information on various family structures: nuclear, extended, single-parent, blended, foster, adoptive, and childless. Organize the class into seven groups reflecting these seven family types. Each group is to prepare a picture collage depicting persons from their assigned type of family. Each group presents their family collage to the class, describing the role of each family member.

Discuss the ways family membership can change. Help the children talk about how this changes the structure of the family group.

Resources Needed: Family magazines for pictures

Evaluation Focus
☒ Knowledge   ☐ Attitude   ☐ Problem Solving

Teacher's Notes (Things to change)

Grade 1 – Family Life Education

Specific Topical Key: Friends

Approximate Time: 50 minutes

Objective

The students will realize that learning to get along with others is a process unique to each individual.

Activities

Lead a discussion with students on the qualities of a friend, such as being trustworthy, respectful, receptive, and reliable. Ask students each to complete a contract to make a new friend.

* *

New Friend Contract

I, _____, on this _____ day of _____ agree to find and make a new friend. I will show that friend that I am dependable, trustworthy, fair, and courteous. I will make sure that I say and do something nice for my new friend. I understand the qualities of a good friend and will demonstrate those qualities by my actions toward those around me.

Signature of student

_____

Signature of new friend

_____

* *

At the next class period, have each student introduce or tell about his or her new friend and share positive comments about that new friend.

Evaluation Focus
□ Knowledge   ⊠ Attitude   □ Problem Solving

Teacher's Notes (Things to change)

Junior High – Family Life Education

Specific Topical Key: Communicating with Parents

Approximate Time: 100 minutes

Objective

The students will recognize the value and necessity of facilitating communication about sexuality with parents.

The students will design an interview questionnaire which can be used by young people to enhance communication with parents.

Activities

Ask students to generate a list of questions like those below to use when interviewing their parents or guardians.

- What was your favorite activity when you were a child?
- What was life like for you when you were a teenager?
- How did you meet each other?
- Where did you go on dates?
- How old were you when you got married?
- What changes occurred when I was born?
- What feelings did you have when I was born?

Then tell students to use the questions developed to interview their parent(s) or guardian(s). Make it clear that they do not necessarily *have* to ask *all* the questions on the list. Also tell them that after everyone has completed the assignment the class will discuss the interviewing and communicating processes, *not* the answers students have gotten to specific questions. *Those answers should be considered private family information.*

When all students have interviewed their parent(s) or guardian(s), discuss the interviewing and communicating processes. This activity could be a good lead-in for a lesson aimed at facilitating communication with parents about sexuality.

Resources Needed: List of questions

Evaluation Focus
    ☐ Knowledge   ☐ Attitude   ☒ Problem Solving

Teacher's Notes (Things to change)

Senior High – Family Life Education

Specific Topical Key: Teenage Pregnancy

Approximate Time: 50 minutes

Objective

The students will recognize problems associated with teenage pregnancy which affect the teenager, friends, family, and community.

Activities

Ask students to talk about how teenagers and others, both male and female, might respond to a hypothetical teenage pregnancy. Together with the class, generate a list of problems associated with teenage pregnancy. Next, have students write reports on the changes, problems, and consequences that would occur in the lives of both teenagers involved as the result of a pregnancy. Tell them to include the implications (physical, social, emotional) for the individuals, friends, family, and community.

Teacher Note: Make sure students know their right to privacy will be respected, and their reports *will not be shared in class discussion.*

Evaluation Focus
☐ Knowledge   ☒ Attitude   ☐ Problem Solving

Teacher's Notes (Things to change)

Mental and Emotional Health

Focus

Topics

Instructional units may be developed for these and other topics related to mental and emotional health: positive self-concept, personality, emotional stability, personal responsibility, motivation, independence, coping with stress, mental health services, goal setting, positive interpersonal relationships, friendships, communication skills, coping with death.

Rationale

Mental or emotional health is not simply the absence of problems. Instead, it is the ability of the individual to use appropriate coping skills to deal with the daily demands of living, skills acceptable both to that individual and to society. It is the ability to experience and express emotions in a positive, stable manner, which demonstrates self-respect and respect for others.

Accidents, homicides, and suicides are the leading causes of death between ages 15 and 24. Many of these deaths have been attributed to behavior patterns characterized by judgmental errors, aggressiveness, and in some cases ambivalence about wanting to live or die. Successful education aimed at promoting positive mental and emotional growth and emphasizing the ability to cope with stress has the potential to prevent many of these problems.

... education aimed at promoting positive mental/emotional growth and emphasizing the ability to cope with stress has the potential to prevent many ... problems.

Life Goals

The individual
- exhibits a positive self-concept;
- expresses emotions comfortably and appropriately;
- weighs potential benefits against possible consequences before choosing one action over another;
- communicates and cooperates effectively with others;
- develops and maintains positive interpersonal relationships.

See also Personal Health, Family Life Education

Kindergarten

Recommended Minimum Time Allocation: eighteen 15-minute periods/ year

By the end of kindergarten, students will
1. value themselves as unique and worthwhile;
2. share with, listen to, and show thoughtfulness and concern for others;
3. know everyone has feelings and that feelings affect behavior;
4. describe "glad," "mad," "sad," and "scared";
5. describe positive ways to express feelings;
6. show ways of coping with upset feelings;
7. recognize how other people influence one's feelings;
8. describe how helping others makes one feel good about oneself;
9. identify persons to go to for help when ill, hurt, concerned, or frightened.

Grade 1

Recommended Minimum Time Allocation: eighteen 25-minute periods/ year

By the end of first grade, students will
1. respect others' rights and property;
2. identify the effects of emotions on the body;
3. differentiate between acceptable and unacceptable behavior;
4. describe positive qualities in themselves and others;
5. recognize that effort is necessary to learn most new skills and to improve old skills;
6. realize that everyone makes mistakes and that people can learn from mistakes;
7. recognize and accept their own abilities and limitations and those of others;
8. describe the importance of belonging to a group and what it feels like to be included or excluded.

Grade 2

Recommended Minimum Time Allocation: eighteen 25-minute periods/year

By the end of second grade, students will
1. differentiate between pleasant and unpleasant emotions;
2. compare responsible with irresponsible expressions of emotion;
3. describe how selected environmental conditions at home or at school can affect how one feels;
4. appreciate their importance to school, family, and peers;
5. know that their behavior does have consequences;
6. appreciate each person's need for time with others and time alone;
7. identify and be sensitive to outward expressions of inner feelings;
8. discuss the different ways people express their feelings.

Grade 3

Recommended Minimum Time Allocation: eighteen 25-minute periods/year

By the end of third grade, students will
1. identify situations in which they might feel glad, mad, sad, or scared;
2. describe how a person's behavior can be helpful or harmful in various situations;
3. identify ways in which physical health affects emotions;
4. define stress and cite examples of positive and negative stressors;
5. identify positive ways of dealing with stress;
6. List behaviors that contribute to and support group membership;
7. identify the factors that enhance or detract from a positive self-image;
8. discuss the similarities of personal loss related to separation by death, separation by divorce, and separation when people move away.

Grade 4

Recommended Minimum Time Allocation: eighteen 25-minute periods/year

By the end of fourth grade, students will
1. demonstrate respect for others' feelings, rights, and property;
2. analyze how a person's self-esteem can be influenced by the actions of others;
3. analyze how one's self-image is influenced by one's own strengths, weaknesses, and accomplishments;
4. discuss the importance of satisfying physical and psychological needs;
5. use communication skills effectively to promote better interpersonal relations;
6. recognize the impact that emotions have on decision making;

7. explain the interrelationship between personal health habits and self-esteem.

Grade 5

Recommended Minimum Time Allocation: thirteen 50-minute periods/year

By the end of fifth grade, students will
1. effectively contribute to positive group decision making;
2. explain the impact of peer influence on behavior;
3. identify and develop effective coping skills;
4. demonstrate interpersonal behaviors which can help people feel comfortable with one another;
5. appreciate that basic emotional needs are the same throughout the life cycle;
6. assess their own attitudes about risk taking;
7. understand some of the factors that motivate their own behavior and that of others;
8. value their personal qualities;
9. differentiate between self-love and selfishness.

Grade 6

Recommended Minimum Time Allocation: fifteen 50-minute periods/year

By the end of sixth grade, students will
1. use a variety of techniques to help them feel good about themselves and to help others feel good about themselves;
2. recognize that common feelings which are expressed or repressed may influence mental health;
3. identify situations that are stress producing;
4. demonstrate the use of decision-making strategies which take into account alternatives, consequences, and optional solutions;
5. analyze how behavior is affected by self-image, values, peers, knowledge, prejudice, ethnic origin, goals, strengths, and weaknesses;
6. explore the value of seeking help for and giving others help with problems and concerns;
7. identify the roles significant people in an individual's life play in providing an emotional and social support system;
8. demonstrate fairness.

Grades 7-8-9, Junior High

Recommended Minimum Time Allocation: *twelve 50-minute periods/semester*

By the end of ninth grade, students will
1. analyze the interrelationships among physical, mental, emotional, and social well-being;
2. demonstrate the ability to set realistic personal goals;
3. consider possible causes and signs of suicide and discuss preventive measures and intervention resources;
4. describe common psychological defense mechanisms;
5. discuss the importance of each individual's setting standards based upon positive emotional-health values;
6. identify those positive personality traits which they desire for themselves and/or observe in others;
7. identify stress management techniques;
8. recognize stages of grief and demonstrate awareness of skills which help people cope with loss;
9. explain known causes of, symptoms of, and ways to prevent eating disorders such as anorexia nervosa and bulimia.

Grades 10-11-12, Senior High

Recommended Minimum Time Allocation: *eight 50-minute periods/semester*

By the end of 12th grade, students will
1. demonstrate the effective communication skills necessary for positive interpersonal relationships;
2. analyze how a satisfying career can contribute to positive interpersonal relationships;
3. explain the relationship of personal strengths and weaknesses to the selection of a satisfying career;
4. formulate a personal plan to maintain their own mental health and to help others stay mentally healthy;
5. demonstrate stress management skills;
6. identify signs of common emotional health problems and list intervention strategies and resources;
7. know about a variety of career choices and occupational opportunities available in the mental and emotional health field.

Grade 1 – Mental and Emotional Health

Specific Topical Key: Self-concept

Approximate Time: 50 minutes

Objective

The students will recognize positive qualities in themselves and others.

Activities

Read the story *The Little Rabbit Who Wanted Red Wings* by Carolyn Sherwin Bailey to your class or, if you prefer, show them the filmstrip that is available.

Afterwards, discuss the book and ask children to fill out the answer sheets.

Script

Do you remember the story of *The Little Rabbit Who Wanted Red Wings?* He always wanted to be anything but what he was. He found out that the best thing to be was himself–a rabbit! There was only one rabbit like him and he decided to be the best he could be. Your job is to be the best that you can be. Just think, there is only one person like you in the whole world. Isn't that great? Now, the little rabbit would like to know more about that special you. Please fill out your answer sheet for him.

Answer Sheet

1) My first name is _____.
2) My last name is _____.
3) I am _____ years old.
4) I am in _____ grade.
5) (Really think about this before you write your answer down.) I am special because

_____

_____.

6) Draw a picture of "that special me."

Teacher Note: This can lead to a discussion about positive qualities others display.

Resources Needed: The book and/or filmstrip entitled *The Little Rabbit Who Wanted Red Wings*.

Evaluation Focus
☐ Knowledge ☒ Attitude ☐ Problem Solving

Teacher's Notes (Things to change)

Grade 5 – Mental and Emotional Health

Specific Topical Key: Peer Pressure

Approximate Time: 50 minutes

Objective

The students will explain the impact of peer influence on behavior.

Activities

Ask for six volunteers from your class to perform the peanut gallery. Give each one of the role descriptions listed below.

Role Descriptions

#1. Eat peanuts slowly and try to get everyone else to enjoy the peanuts.

#2. You will be offered peanuts by #1 and even though you will say they are not good for you, you will accept. Take your time eating them. Then help convince others to enjoy them.

#3. Others will try to persuade you to eat the peanuts. Resist their claims. Wait a while, then give in.

#4. Others will try to persuade you to eat the peanuts. Resist their claims. Wait a while, then give in.

#5. The others will try to pressure you. No matter what, do not take any peanuts.

#6. No matter what, do not take any peanuts.

Give character #1 the peanuts and let the activity progress. The activity should conclude after #3 and #4 have joined characters #1 and #2 in eating peanuts.

Discussion Questions

1) How did you feel about being pressured to do something when you kept saying "No, I won't!"? (#5/6)
2) How did you feel when you resisted? (#3/4)
3) How did you feel when you gave in? (#3/4)
4) How did you feel when #2 gave in and started pressuring you? (#3/4)
5) How did you feel about pressuring the others? Was it easier when #2 joined you? (#1)
6) How did you feel while watching the participants? (class)
7) Why do people pressure others into making decisions? (class)
8) What can you do to resist peer pressure to make decisions that you don't want to make? (class)

Source: *Here's Looking at You, Two,* Comprehensive Health Education Foundation, Seattle, WA

Resources Needed: Peanuts, role descriptions

Evaluation Focus
  ☐ Knowledge   ☒ Attitude   ☒ Problem Solving

Teacher's Notes (Things to change)

Junior High – Mental and Emotional Health

Specific Topical Key: Self-concept

Approximate Time: 50 minutes

Objective

The students will identify those positive personality traits which they desire for themselves and/or observe in others.

Activities

The teacher leads a discussion about qualities students admire most in their classmates and desire for themselves. Following the discussion, the class forms a circle (including the teacher) and remains standing. Each student is given a 3" by 5" note card. Each student, along with the teacher, print his or her name across the middle of the card, and holds the card face down. The teacher says, "Pass your card to the right and take one from the left." This is repeated several times so that the cards are randomly distributed. When the teacher says "Stop," each student turns over the card he/she holds and writes several honest, positive comments about the person whose name appears on the card.

This process continues until the cards are full of positive comments. If the students receive their own cards or ones they have already had, they should exchange with someone else. Finally, each card is returned to the person whose name is on it.

Each student looks at his or her own card and circles what each considers his or her two best qualities. Each student may wish to share his or her card with a boy and a girl in the class.

Teacher Note: Tell the students to keep their cards in their notebooks so they can refer to the cards when they need an emotional lift.

Evaluation Focus
　☐ Knowledge　　　☒ Attitude　　　☐ Problem Solving

Teacher's Notes (Things to change)

Senior High – Mental and Emotional Health

Specific Topical Key: Communication

Approximate Time: 50 minutes

Objective

The students will demonstrate the effective communications skills necessary for positive interpersonal relationships.

Activities

Students and teacher sit in one large circle. The students are asked to answer in turn a set of general-interest questions as an introductory activity. Then, when each has spoken, the teacher asks various persons at random to repeat what another in the circle has said. This activity can be used to spark discussion as to which persons are the most skillful listeners and the importance of both listening and speaking for effective communication.

The students are then taught the basic concepts of reflective listening, learning first to accurately restate what another has said and then to reflect on and express the underlying feelings.

Then students can practice listening and making reflective responses in pairs or small groups.

Evaluation Focus
⊠ Knowledge   ☐ Attitude   ⊠ Problem Solving

Teacher's Notes (Things to change)

Nutrition

9

Focus

Topics

Instructional units may be developed for these and other topics related to nutrition: food choices, elements in food that contribute to good nutrition, factors influencing choices, individual nutritional requirements, food groups and nutrients, food sources, diet and weight control, effects of nutrition on growth and activity, consumer protection, positive eating plans.

Rationale

Food habits which help build and protect good health are not acquired naturally; they must be learned.

Several recent studies of nutritional status and food consumption suggest that many Americans are not making well-informed choices. Young children, teenagers, pregnant women, and the elderly are most vulnerable to the effects of an inadequate diet. According to estimates, 15 million Americans are sufficiently overweight to impair their health.

Food habits which help build and protect good health are not acquired naturally; they must be learned. It is important for students to be provided with nutrition knowledge and training during their early school years.

Life Goals

The individual
- eats a daily diet that provides adequate nutrients for the maintenance of health;
- selects a wide range of foodstuffs;
- balances calorie intake with energy needs.

Student Objectives

See also Consumer Health, Personal Health, Prevention and Control of Disease

Special note: See Nutrition in Health – An Instructional Package for Grades K–6.

90

Kindergarten

Recommended Minimum Time Allocation: eighteen 15-minute periods/ year

By the end of kindergarten, students will
1. recognize the importance of eating breakfast;
2. identify nutritious snacks;
3. prepare a simple snack or meal;
4. discriminate between food and nonfood items;
5. recognize factors used in advertisements to sell food products.

Grade 1

Recommended Minimum Time Allocation: eighteen 25-minute periods/ year

By the end of first grade, students will
1. identify sensory characteristics of foods;
2. classify plant and animal sources of food;
3. identify food in different forms;
4. trace a food from origin to table;
5. demonstrate good mealtime manners;
6. recognize the importance of eating a variety of foods from several food groups.

Grade 2

Recommended Minimum Time Allocation: eighteen 25-minute periods/ year

By the end of second grade, students will
1. indicate that people need food from a variety of sources for energy, growth, maintenance, and repair;
2. describe ways the body uses and stores energy;
3. evaluate their own diets to identify reasons for food choices;
4. describe factors that promote dental caries;
5. identify sources of sugar in the diet;
6. recognize significance of order of ingredients on food labels;
7. compare varying amounts of nutrients and energy needed throughout the life cycle.

Grade 3

Recommended Minimum Time Allocation: eighteen 25-minute periods/ year

By the end of third grade, students will
1. describe how family, friends, and peers influence food choices;
2. give examples of how sensory qualities of food affect food choices;
3. identify how emotions influence eating behavior;
4. state that food supplies nutrients needed for growth, repair, and maintenance of cells;
5. know that energy from the sun is converted to food energy by plants;
6. identify the energy needs of persons involved in various activities;
7. construct a food chain when given food sources.

Grade 4

Recommended Minimum Time Allocation: eighteen 25-minute periods/ year

By the end of fourth grade, students will
1. define "nutrient";
2. identify the major classes of nutrients and their functions;
3. define "calorie";
4. discuss factors such as age, body size, activity level, and physical condition that affect basic nutrient and energy requirements;
5. recognize and practice positive activities aimed at maintaining their ideal weight;
6. identify reliable sources of food and nutrition information.

Grade 5

Recommended Minimum Time Allocation: ten 50-minute periods/year

By the end of fifth grade, students will
1. identify major sources of key nutrients;
2. classify foods into groups based on their major nutrient contributions to the diet;
3. identify portion sizes and number of servings suggested within each food group to meet Recommended Dietary Allowances;
4. suggest methods to identify the amounts of sugars, sodium, and fats consumed;
5. recognize relationships between diet and blood pressure;
6. recognize the sources and importance of fiber;
7. appreciate the importance and social value of eating with others;
8. evaluate sample menus in terms of food groups, nutrients, and calories.

Grade 6

Recommended Minimum Time Allocation: ten 50-minute periods/year

By the end of sixth grade, students will
1. compare nutrient density of foods;
2. assess the nutritional components of their diets;
3. discuss ways to prevent deficiencies or excesses of key nutrients;
4. give examples of how economics influence food prices, availability, and promotional strategies;
5. recognize the relationships between diet and the body systems;
6. plan a day's diet that contains amounts of key nutrients required within their energy needs.

Grades 7-8-9, Junior High

Recommended Minimum Time Allocation: five 50-minute periods/ semester

By the end of ninth grade, students will
1. assess the health impact of a variety of diets;
2. develop a positive eating plan that takes into account sugar, sodium, fat, other nutrients, and fiber content;
3. identify factors affecting basic nutrient and energy requirements and compute caloric needs for various activities, lifestyles, and states of health;
4. know about a variety of career choices and occupational opportunities available in the area of nutrition and health.

Grades 10-11-12, Senior High

Recommended Minimum Time Allocation: five 50-minute periods/ semester

By the end of 12th grade, students will
1. construct within a specified budget, a weekly diet using locally available foods;
2. evaluate a diet by identifying sugar, sodium, fat, other nutrients, and fiber content;
3. compare the nutritional value and effects on health of food supplements and additives.

Kindergarten – Nutrition

Specific Topical Key: Breakfast

Approximate Time: 90 minutes

Objectives

The students will state the importance of eating breakfast.

The students will realize that, like all fuel, food is used up by the body and must be constantly supplied.

Activities

For the first part of this activity, have students sit in a large circle on the floor. You should sit in the circle with them.

Wind up a small plastic or metal toy loosely (a few cranks) and before placing it near the middle of the circle for all to see, tell your students to carefully observe what happens to it. When the toy stops, ask the students what happened. Ask them what you could do to make it move again. Then wind up the toy and set it in motion, *but* catch it before it completely runs down. Quickly rewind the toy to keep it in continuous motion.

Tell the students that their bodies are something like the toy, in that their bodies can work for hours, but eventually they run down and must be "wound up" again. Ask the students how bodies get wound up. State that *food*, eaten at different times of the day, keeps our energy levels high and our bodies wound up so that we can work and play without having to stop.

Ask students when they eat during the day. Have them name the three main meals of the day—breakfast, lunch, and supper.

Ask students why eating just once a day won't last us all day long. (The body needs to be refueled or wound up every few hours to keep going strong.)

Ask students how they might know when they are starting to run out of energy. They feel hungry. They get tired, their stomachs rumble, and so on.

Now stress that there is a *long* time between supper and breakfast. Emphasize that, like the toy which they saw run down, their bodies run out of energy overnight and need to be refueled, or wound up, at breakfast.

Pass out paper and crayons. Have each child draw a picture of his or her favorite nutritious breakfast. Have them include foods they eat and drink. After they are finished drawing, ask students to share their pictures with each other. While sitting in a circle, the students can take turns holding up their drawings and presenting the following information: a) breakfast food choices on the drawing, b) who usually makes their breakfasts at home, and c) whether or not they eat breakfast every morning.

Make a bulletin board display of the breakfast drawings.

Source: *Nutrition in Health: An Instructional Package for Grades K–6*, Wisconsin Department of Public Instruction, Madison.

Resources Needed: Small plastic or metal wind-up toy

Evaluation Focus
    ☒ Knowledge   ☒ Attitude   ☐ Problem Solving

Teacher's Notes (Things to change)

Grade 4 – Nutrition

Specific Topical Key: Energy Balance

Approximate Time: 100 minutes

Objectives

The students will discuss factors such as age, body size, activity level, and physical condition that affect basic nutrient and energy requirements.

The students will recognize that the amount of food energy a person takes in should match the amount of energy expended.

Activities

Begin by asking your students if they know about how much food they need to eat on a daily basis. Tell them that energy is derived from the food people eat and that people burn up energy all day long. Mention that the amount of energy everyone gets from the foods they eat should approximately equal the amount of energy used up in their daily activities.

Explain to students that they should know roughly about how much energy (calories) they need to get from their food. There are official government estimates of how many calories people need each day; these are called Recommended Dietary Allowances (RDA).

Pass out copies of "Recommended Dietary Allowances." Instruct students to use the chart to find out how many calories they need in a day. Have students compare their energy requirements.

Stress that the figures on the energy requirement chart are averages; *everybody is different!* The information on the handout is a general guideline, not an absolute rule. Mention to the class that there are a number of factors affecting the energy requirements of different people—age, body size, activity level, and physiological state (that is, growth, pregnancy, and so on).

Explain to the students that they are now going to get an idea of the calorie content, or energy value, of some of their favorite foods. Distribute copies of the handout "Edible Energy" chart and discuss the caloric values of: a) skim milk versus chocolate milkshake, b) french fries versus mashed potatoes, c) white bread versus white toast, d) plain popcorn versus potato chips.

Hand out copies of the "Expendable Energy" chart and discuss the relationship of caloric intake to energy expended in a variety of physical activities.

Distribute copies of the "C-Saw" worksheet. Go over the directions aloud and give students 15 minutes to complete the sheet. Discuss completed sheets during class or have them submitted to you for comments.

Source: *Nutrition in Health: An Instructional Package for Grades K–6,* Wisconsin Department of Public Instruction, Madison.

Resources Needed: Attached handouts (4)

Evaluation Focus
   ☒ Knowledge   ☐ Attitude   ☒ Problem Solving

Teacher's Notes (Things to change)

Grade 4 – Nutrition/Handout
Recommended Dietary Allowances

	AGE	WEIGHT (Pounds)	HEIGHT (Inches)	ENERGY (Calories)
CHILDREN				
	1 - 3	28	34	1300
	4 - 6	44	44	1700
	7 - 10	66	54	2400
MALES	11 - 14	97	63	2700
	15 - 18	134	69	2800
	19 - 22	147	69	2900
	23 - 50	154	69	2700
	51 +	154	69	2400
FEMALES	11 - 14	97	62	2200
	15 - 18	119	65	2100
	19 - 22	128	65	2100
	23 - 50	128	65	2000
	51 +	128	65	1800

Grade 4 – Nutrition/Handout
Edible Energy

Milk Group	AMOUNT	CALORIES
American Cheese	1 oz.	106
Chocolate Milkshake	$1\frac{1}{3}$ cups	356
Ice Cream	$\frac{1}{2}$ cup	135
Skim Milk	1 cup	86
Strawberry Yogurt	1 cup	225
Whole Milk	1 cup	150
Meat Group		
Beef Roast	3 oz.	182
Fried Chicken	3 oz.	201
Fried Egg	large	83
Hamburger	3 oz.	186
Peanut Butter	2 Tbsp.	186
Tuna Fish	3 oz.	180
Fruit–Vegetable Group		
Apple	medium	80
Banana	medium	101
Corn	$\frac{1}{2}$ cup	70
French Fries	20	233
Green Beans	$\frac{1}{2}$ cup	16
Mashed Potatoes	$\frac{1}{2}$ cup	63
Orange Juice	$\frac{1}{2}$ cup	56
Tossed Salad	$\frac{3}{4}$ cup	13
Grain Group		
Cornflakes	$\frac{3}{4}$ cup	72
Hamburger Roll	one	119
White Bread	slice	61
White Toast	slice	61
Whole Wheat Bread	slice	55
Combination Foods		
Beef Taco	one	216
Cheese Pizza	$\frac{1}{4}$ of 14"	354
Others		
Butter	1 tsp.	36
French Dressing	1 Tbsp.	66
Milk Chocolate Bar	1 oz.	147
Plain Popcorn	1 cup	23
Potato Chips	10	114
Soft Drink (Cola)	$1\frac{1}{2}$ cups	150

Grade 4 – Nutrition/Handout
Expendable Energy

ACTIVITY	ENERGY USED PER HOUR
Quiet Things: Watching TV, eating, reading, playing cards.	80 - 100 Calories
Light Activities: Walking slowly, practicing a musical instrument, doing dishes.	110 - 160 Calories
Medium Things: Cleaning up your room (really cleaning it!), walking pretty fast, household chores, bowling, ping-pong	170 - 240 Calories
Active Things: Bike riding, tennis, hiking, jogging, hockey, soccer, swimming	250 - 350 Calories

Grade 4 – Nutrition/Handout
C–Saw: The Balancing Act You Perform!

C = calorie

Directions. Balance the activity on the left side of each C-Saw with an appropriate snack choice (see lists below). Write your snack choice on the right side of the C-Saw. You should use your two handouts – Edible Energy and Expendable Energy.

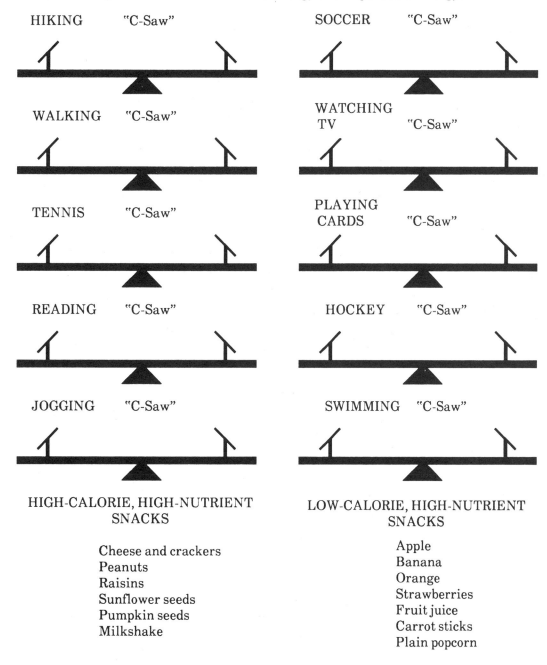

HIKING   "C-Saw"

SOCCER   "C-Saw"

WALKING   "C-Saw"

WATCHING TV   "C-Saw"

TENNIS   "C-Saw"

PLAYING CARDS   "C-Saw"

READING   "C-Saw"

HOCKEY   "C-Saw"

JOGGING   "C-Saw"

SWIMMING   "C-Saw"

HIGH-CALORIE, HIGH-NUTRIENT SNACKS

Cheese and crackers
Peanuts
Raisins
Sunflower seeds
Pumpkin seeds
Milkshake

LOW-CALORIE, HIGH-NUTRIENT SNACKS

Apple
Banana
Orange
Strawberries
Fruit juice
Carrot sticks
Plain popcorn

Junior High – Nutrition

Specific Topical Key: Personal Eating Plan

Approximate Time: 100 minutes (ongoing)

Objectives

Students will develop a positive eating plan that takes into account sugar, sodium, fat, other nutrients, and fiber content.
● Students will use information on food labels to compare the ingredients and nutritional value of high-sugar and unenriched grain products.
● Students will suggest ways to substitute more nutritious foods for high-sugar and unenriched grain products in their diets.

Activities

Collect front and back labels, complete wrappers, or boxes or containers from "sugar" products—candies, jams, jellies, flavored gelatins, toppings, syrups. Also collect them from unenriched grain products like bagels, buns, some macaroni-type foods, and any other grain products with labels that say "unenriched" or that don't specifically say "enriched" if whole-grain flour is missing. Mount or staple them on sheets of paper so that backs and fronts do not get separated and so they are easy to store. Students may wish to help collection and mounting.

Pass the label sheets around in class. Ask students to look at all the labels and identify similarities among products. They should find that

1) carbohydrate—starch or sugar—is a major ingredient (energy source) in all;
2) all contain few or no minerals, vitamins, protein;
3) the number of calories per serving is relatively large, especially for sugar products;
4) for those with "pull date" information, expected shelf life is long.

Note: If labels list only the ingredients, this gives students less information. They may only be able to deduce that sugar or starch is the main ingredient in the products selected. Thus, it would be more educational to include as many labels with nutrition information as possible.

Discuss positive and negative aspects of these foods. Some of them are listed below.

Positive

Sugar makes food taste good.
Carmel (sugar) adds texture and color to bakery products.
Sugars help thicken, firm, or preserve foods.
Unenriched products may cost less.

Negative

Sugars offer little nutritionally except calories.

Sugars and unenriched grain products replace other foods that do contain minerals, vitamins, and protein.

Sugars add calories without bulk or fiber.

Sugar's extra calories can cause weight gain.

Sugar is major contributing factor to dental caries (cavities).

Ask students to suggest ways to substitute other more nutritious foods in their diets. Below are some suggestions.

- Always check the labels for "enriched" grain products.
- Use fresh fruit or low-sugar preserves.
- Eat fresh or roasted nuts rather than candy.
- Make sundaes with fresh fruit instead of prepared toppings.
- Use more whole-grain products, which do not need enrichment.
- At the bakery, ask if products are enriched.

Source: *Nutrition in Teenage Pregnancy,* Wisconsin Department of Public Instruction, Madison

Resources Needed: Labels and wrappers

Evaluation Focus

    ☒ Knowledge   ☒ Attitude   ☒ Problem Solving

Teacher's Notes (Things to change)

Senior High – Nutrition

Specific Topical Key: Diet Evaluation

Approximate Time: 50 minutes

Objective

The student will evaluate a diet by identifying sugar, sodium, fat (saturated and unsaturated), other nutrients, and fiber content.

Activities

Students are to plan and implement a series of cafeteria meals focusing on fiber, sodium, sugar and/or fat content.

Arrange with school food services to have a series of "Health Day Meals" (perhaps one per month), with themes like Cut Down on Sugar, Meals with Less Fat, Why Add Salt, Fiber for Health. Divide class into small groups. Each month one group should help plan a meal with the food service staff and prepare a brief one-page announcement of the meal and nutrition theme, explaining the benefits of each food available. Groups should build up interest in the meal through PA announcements, posters, table tents in the cafeteria, and so on.

Evaluation Focus

☒ Knowledge   ☒ Attitude   ☒ Problem Solving

Teacher's Notes (Things to change)

Personal Health

10

Focus
Student Objectives
Sample Lessons

Focus

Topics

Instructional units may be developed for these and other topics related to personal health: physical fitness and lifetime activities, cardiovascular health, sleep, rest, relaxation, recreation, growth and development, oral health, vision and hearing, body systems and their functions, aging, personal wellness plans, positive health habits and choices.

Rationale

The realization that each person is largely responsible for the status of his/her own health is a significant step in achieving and maintaining fitness and total well-being.

The state of a person's health is invariably the result of the interplay among three major factors: environment, heredity, and personal lifestyle. Of these, it is through lifestyle—habits and behaviors—that a person directly influences the state of his or her own health.

Mortality data indicate the importance of lifestyle. Of the ten leading causes of death in the United States, at least seven could be reduced substantially if persons at risk changed their health behavior. The realization that each person is largely responsible for the status of his or her own health is a significant step in achieving and maintaining fitness and total well-being.

Life Goals

The individual
- adheres to a health promotion/wellness-oriented lifestyle;
- pursues leisure-time activities that promote physical fitness and relieve stress and emotional tension;
- follows health care practices that prevent illness and maintain health.

Student Objectives

See also Mental and Emotional Health, Family Life Education
Special Note: See A Guide to Curriculum Planning in Physical Education.

Kindergarten

Recommended Minimum Time Allocation: eighteen 15-minute periods/ year

By the end of kindergarten, students will

1. describe factors which promote health, growth, and good feelings about self;
2. demonstrate a willingness to balance regular, vigorous activities with rest and relaxation;
3. begin assuming responsibility for personal grooming and cleanliness habits;
4. demonstrate ways to care for teeth, including brushing and flossing;
5. demonstrate healthful sitting and standing postures;
6. know that living organisms come from other living organisms.

Grade 1

Recommended Minimum Time Allocation: eighteen 25-minute periods/ year

By the end of first grade, students will

1. demonstrate knowledge of activities which help promote personal cleanliness, improve appearance, and reduce transmission of disease;
2. recognize the relationship between physical activity and muscular development;
3. know the function of the heart;
4. give personal examples that illustrate the relationship between physical and mental health;
5. identify types, functions, and care of teeth;
6. be able to recognize when they are tired or fatigued and identify ways to rest and relax;
7. recognize that the brain directs all activities of the body;
8. identify the human senses.

Grade 2

Recommended Minimum Time Allocation: eighteen 25-minute periods/ year

By the end of second grade, students will

1. cite examples of the ways individuals grow physically, socially, emotionally, and mentally;
2. discover that decision making is involved in choosing and assessing personal health practices;
3. identify, locate, and describe the major organs in the human body;
4. value physical well-being by practicing fitness behaviors which contribute to health;
5. recognize that the heart is a muscle that is strengthened by exercise;
6. recognize the need for rest and quiet activities;
7. demonstrate health and safety practices for each of the human senses.

Grade 3

Recommended Minimum Time Allocation: eighteen 25-minute periods/ year

By the end of third grade, students will
1. demonstrate the ability to make positive health and lifestyle decisions;
2. explain how health affects performance;
3. tell how good posture affects the body and self-image;
4. recognize the need to rest the muscles;
5. illustrate how emotions are revealed through physical actions;
6. cite ways to build physical activities into daily routine;
7. name and identify the main parts of the sense organs and their functions;
8. appreciate the contributions of the sense organs to safety, learning, and play;
9. describe the general structure and function of the body systems;
10. demonstrate good dental habits, including a review of correct brushing and flossing techniques;
11. recognize and accept individual differences, including personal handicapping conditions.

Grade 4

Recommended Minimum Time Allocation: eighteen 25-minute periods/ year

By the end of fourth grade, students will
1. recognize that total health is both a condition and a process;
2. investigate how individuals can utilize work, rest, sleep, exercise, good posture, play, and nutrition to promote well-being;
3. develop plans for rewarding themselves for positive health behaviors;
4. recognize the need to set priorities for personal health activities;
5. accept that each individual has a unique rate of growth and development;
6. define and identify inherited characteristics;
7. describe the basic mechanics of the circulatory system.

Grade 5

Recommended Minimum Time Allocation: thirteen 50-minute periods/ year

By the end of fifth grade, students will
1. recognize the effects personal health practices have on social, mental, emotional, and physical well-being;

2. investigate functions of the body systems and identify major organs in each system;
3. describe ways in which the body systems are interdependent;
4. appreciate the effects of diet and exercise on body composition;
5. identify benefits of both aerobic and anaerobic exercise;
6. identify characteristics of puberty and the effects of these changes on physical, emotional, and social development.

Grade 6

Recommended Minimum Time Allocation: twelve 50-minute periods/year

By the end of sixth grade, students will
1. recognize that healthy lifestyles have several components, such as personal responsibility, stress management, nutrition, physical fitness, and environmental sensitivity;
2. describe the basic structure and function of a cell;
3. show they know the benefits of meeting individual needs for rest and sleep;
4. appreciate the effect of grooming on interpersonal relationships;
5. recognize the importance of establishing an ongoing and effective exercise plan which meets personal requirements and accommodates limitations.

Grades 7-8-9, Junior High

Recommended Minimum Time Allocation: ten 50-minute periods/semester

By the end of ninth grade, students will
1. describe health care practices during adolescence that may follow from various individual decisions;
2. recognize the impact health habits have on stress levels;
3. demonstrate appropriate stress management techniques;
4. analyze fad behavior as a force affecting health decisions;
5. describe some common causes of skin problems and suggest procedures for good skin care;
6. interpret the results of a credible health hazard appraisal (wellness inventory) in behavioral terms.

Grades 10-11-12, Senior High

Recommended Minimum Time Allocation: nine 50-minute periods/ semester

By the end of 12th grade, students will
1. recognize that there is an interrelationship among physical, mental, emotional, and social factors which determines levels of well-being;

2. design and implement a personal health plan adaptable to changing lifelong needs;
3. recognize social forces and norms that exert positive or negative influences on health practices, including fitness and diet;
4. apply principles of energy balance to the planning of a diet and activity pattern which will result in healthy body weight and composition;
5. appreciate and demonstrate the impact significant people have on the health lifestyles of others;
6. know about a wide variety of career choices and occupational opportunities available in personal health promotion and fitness.

Grade 1 – Personal Health

Specific Topical Key: Dental Health

Approximate Time: 25 minutes

Objective

The students will identify types, functions, and care of teeth.

Activities

Construct the bulletin board described below. Label it "What Makes Your Teeth Happy or Sad?"

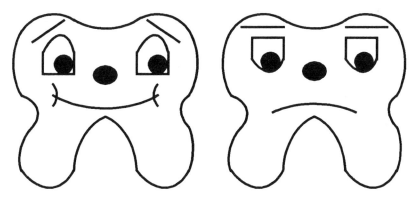

Cut out two big teeth, one happy and one sad. Have children cut pictures out of magazines that make teeth happy or sad and paste on the teeth. For example, apples and toothbrush go on the happy tooth, and candy and soda go on the sad tooth. Students may also *draw* pictures and paste them on the teeth.

Also, have the children make tooth puppets and present plays. One puppet is happy and one is sad. What should the teeth say? Why are they happy or sad? (Two-people play: one happy and one sad.)

Source: Diane Wedl, Johnson Creek Elementary School

Evaluation Focus
☒ Knowledge   ☒ Attitude   ☐ Problem Solving

Teacher's Notes (Things to change)

Grade 4 – Personal Health

Specific Topical Key: Family Tree of Heights

Approximate Time: 25 minutes

Objectives:

The students will define and identify inherited characteristics.

Activities

Students will construct a family "height" tree, with spaces for names and heights of blood relatives, present and previous generations where possible. Students are responsible for obtaining accurate measurements of the heights of all available family members.

When trees are completed, students will return the results to class for a discussion of inherited characteristics, and what personal predictions they can make based on their families' inherited characteristics. The discussion should cover the effects of inherited characteristics on personal health.

This activity could be expanded to include other inherited characteristics such as eye color, hair type, and so on.

Evaluation Focus

☒ Knowledge   ☐ Attitude   ☒ Problem Solving

Teacher's Notes (Things to change)

Specific Topical Key: Stress Management

Approximate Time: 50 minutes

Objectives

The students will demonstrate appropriate stress management techniques.

Activities

Students place temperature strips or biofeedback devices on their hands. After an explanation of how stress affects the temperature of the hand, students are exposed to a variety of stressors, for example, giving a short speech, hearing a startling noise, or high-volume music, and note the effects on their temperatures. For contrast, students then participate in a relaxation exercise, which might be listening to measured, soft music, visualization, or a deep-breathing activity. Again, students observe the effect upon their temperatures. A discussion can help to generalize these observations to the effects of everyday situations which may be stressful.

Resources Needed: Temperature strips or biofeedback cards (one source: University of Wisconsin–LaCrosse Health Education Department).

Evaluation Focus
☒ Knowledge ☐ Attitude ☒ Problem Solving

Teacher's Notes (Things to change)

Senior High – Personal Health

Specific Topical Key: Personal Wellness Contract

Approximate Time: 50 minutes

Objectives

The students will design and implement a personal health plan adaptable to changing lifelong needs.

Activities

Pair two students who are each interested in changing a health behavior and in helping one another with the process.

Ask each person to specify what he or she wants from the contract, and what each will do to get it. A sharing of ideas, fairness, and mutual compromise are needed to accomplish this task.

Include in the contract a set of consequences for compliance and noncompliance. Compliance should result in a reward. Failure to comply with the contract can be followed by a penalty, though punishments should be avoided.

Formalize the agreement by putting it in writing and having each party sign it.

Below are rules to follow for contract development.
- Goals should be realistic and short term.
- When goals are met, students should be rewarded immediately.
- Rewards should be given after positive behavior change occurs.
- Contract terms must be clear, fair, and positive.
- Contract must be consistent and not renegotiated until an agreed-upon time by both parties.

Source: Tom Kidd, Osseo-Fairchild and Fall Creek Public Schools

Evaluation Focus
☐ Knowledge ☒ Attitude ☒ Problem Solving

Teacher's Notes (Things to change)

Senior High – Personal Health/ Personal Wellness Contract Being My Own Best Friend

Student Goal. I plan to take responsibility for enhancing my personal wellness this semester by making the following changes:

To realistically accomplish my goal, I commit myself to taking the following steps.

Date to be completed

Step 1

Step 2

Step 3

Step 4

Step 5

I realize that it's easy to fool myself and put things off; therefore, I need to keep the following "cop-outs" in mind.

I feel my classmates would see this change in me as:

Upon reaching my goal, I plan to reward myself by:

_____

(signature of student)

Witness: I agree to meet with _____
on _____, 19____ to evaluate the completion of this contract and/or to
discuss problems encountered and renegotiate if necessary.

_____

(signature of witness)

115

Prevention and Control of Disease

Focus
Student Objectives
Sample Lessons

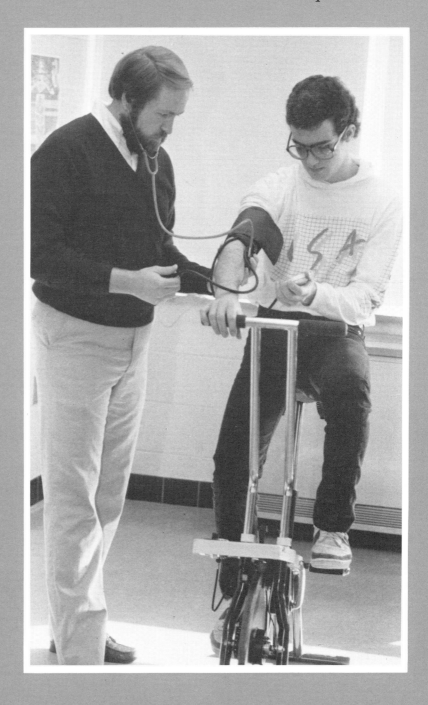

Focus

Topics

Instructional units may be developed for these and other topics related to prevention and control of disease: causes of disease, preventive measures, chronic disease, degenerative disease, communicable disease, immunization, personal health practices, community efforts, personal responsibility, career opportunities.

Rationale

Everyone from birth onward is sometimes exposed to disease or at risk for developing a health problem. Factors such as heredity, socioeconomic background, prenatal exposure, environment, and behavior influence each person's degree of risk for developing particular diseases. Also, two or more risk factors may interact, reinforcing and multiplying their effects.

Medical advances have dramatically decreased the mortality rate due to major infections, but there has been a 250-percent increase in the number of fatalities caused by major chronic diseases. There is increasing evidence that the roots of these adult chronic diseases, for example, heart disease, stroke, diabetes, cancer, may be found in early life.

Eating patterns, exercise habits, and exposure to cancer-causing substances can all increase the individual's potential for developing disease in later life. Yet changes in personal behavior are difficult to attain when health benefits are not visible in the short term. Students should learn to protect themselves and others from disease and should form health-enhancing habits.

Students should learn to protect themselves and others from disease and should form health-enhancing habits.

Life Goals

The individual
- adheres to a lifestyle that promotes well-being and minimizes exposure to known risk factors;
- maintains immunizations of self and family at recommended levels of effectiveness;
- takes preventive measures, such as going for health examinations at specified intervals.

118

See also Community Health, Environmental Health, Consumer Health, Nutrition.

Kindergarten

Recommended Minimum Time Allocation: six 15-minute periods/year

By the end of kindergarten, students will
1. compare how people look and feel when well and ill;
2. suggest behaviors associated with feeling well and ill;
3. know proper clothing to wear for various weather conditions and its relationship to prevention of disease;
4. know the value of good personal hygiene habits.

Grade 1

Recommended Minimum Time Allocation: six 15-minute periods/year

By the end of first grade, students will
1. express the idea that each person is well most of the time;
2. describe and appreciate what it feels like to be well;
3. discuss the relationship between germs and disease;
4. suggest ways to prevent illness;
5. recognize and appreciate medical personnel and the purpose of medicine;
6. recognize public health efforts aimed at prevention and control of disease.

Grade 2

Recommended Minimum Time Allocation: six 15-minute periods/year

By the end of second grade, students will
1. suggest and demonstrate behaviors which help prevent disease and encourage well-being;
2. appreciate and value behaviors which will help prevent disease, such as exercising, eating properly, getting enough rest, and maintaining personal hygiene;
3. describe how germs cause illness;
4. explain how communicable diseases spread;
5. recognize the value of immunization as a personal protection and a community benefit.

Grade 3

Recommended Minimum Time Allocation: six 15-minute periods/year

By the end of third grade, students will
1. evaluate their health behaviors in terms of health promotion and disease prevention;
2. distinguish between infectious and noninfectious disease;
3. describe disease symptoms and steps to take when these symptoms first appear;
4. identify habits that may increase risk of disease;
5. recognize the physical, emotional, and social characteristics of a healthy lifestyle.

Grade 4

Recommended Minimum Time Allocation: six 15-minute periods/year

By the end of fourth grade, students will
1. know and appreciate the relationship between personal behavior and health or illness;
2. describe how heredity and environment influence health status;
3. recognize that many diseases can be avoided, delayed, or minimized by use of positive health practices;
4. appreciate the importance of personal responsibility for avoiding and/or minimizing disease;
5. recognize the roles of parents, friends and health care professionals in enhancing health and preventing and treating disease.

Grade 5

Recommended Minimum Time Allocation: three 50-minute periods/year

By the end of fifth grade, students will
1. develop a personal plan for avoiding disease and enhancing health;
2. explain the process of communicable disease transmission;
3. describe personal and social factors that motivate their health behavior.

Grade 6

Recommended Minimum Time Allocation: three 50-minute periods/year

By the end of sixth grade, students will
1. evaluate their own health practices and describe the immediate consequences of positive and negative health behaviors;
2. explain the relationship between the human immune system and the disease process;

3. name the four major killers of Americans today.

Grades 7-8-9, Junior High

Recommended Minimum Time Allocation: three 50-minute periods/ semester

By the end of ninth grade, students will
1. evaluate their past and present health practices and design positive changes for the future;
2. determine the hereditary, environmental, and lifestyle factors which place them at risk for disease and/or enhance their health;
3. identify sources, symptoms, and treatments of sexually transmitted diseases.

Grades 10-11-12, Senior High

Recommended Minimum Time Allocation: four 50-minute periods/ semester

By the end of 12th grade, students will
1. explain causes, symptoms, and ways to prevent infectious mono-nucleosis;
2. identify agencies that treat communicable diseases or chronic disorders and describe their referral procedures;
3. design a plan aimed at disease prevention and health promotion for themselves, their families, and the community;
4. know about a variety of career choices and occupational opportunities available in disease prevention and control.

Grade 2 – Prevention and Control of Disease

Specific Topical Key: Behaviors for Well-being

Approximate Time: Ongoing

Objective

The students will suggest and demonstrate behaviors which help prevent disease and encourage well-being.

Activities

Review and discuss healthy before-school routines, such as eating breakfast, washing face and hands, brushing teeth and making someone happy. Point out the reason for each routine, that is, how it helps prevent disease and encourage well-being. Pass out the worksheet entitled "A Healthy Routine Before School."

Explain the activity to the students. As the child does each activity each morning, the parents put a "happy face" in the appropriate box. If an activity is not done, then a sad face is put in the appropriate box. The parents sign the sheet each week. The sheet is passed out each Friday afternoon and returned to school the following Friday morning. The students receive a wellness or health certificate each time they return the sheet completed and signed by their parents.

This activity can be continued during the second semester with the "Healthy Routine After School" sheet.

Source: Diane Wedl, Johnson Creek Elementary School

Resources Needed: "Routine" worksheets and wellness certificates

Evaluation Focus
    ☒ Knowledge   ☒ Attitude   ☒ Problem Solving

Teacher's Notes (Things to change)

Grade 2 – Prevention and Control of Disease/Worksheet
A Healthy Routine before School

Name _____

Week of _____

	Monday	Tuesday	Wednesday	Thursday	Friday
Eat Breakfast					
Brush Teeth					
Wash Face & Hands					
Make Someone Happy					

Parent's Signature _____

Grade 2 – Prevention and Control of Disease/Worksheet
A Healthy Routine after School

Name _____

Week of _____

	Monday	Tuesday	Wednesday	Thursday	Friday
Did school work					
Ate dinner	I HAD _____ _____ _____				
Had fun with someone (Sharing is fun!)					
Brushed teeth before bed					
Went to bed	I WENT TO BED AT _____				

Parent's Signature _____

Grade 6 – Prevention and Control of Disease

Specific Topical Key: Major Killers

Approximate Time: 50 minutes

Objective

The students will name the four major killers of Americans today.

Activities

Following a lecture on the four major killers of Americans—heart disease, cancer, stroke, and accidents—the students will create an advertising campaign with the theme "May the 'Fours' Not Be with You."

The students can work in pairs to construct posters advertising the healthy behaviors that can help prevent the four major killers. Encourage the students to use the *Star Wars* theme to add drama and flair to their advertisements.

Source: Jon Hisgen, School District of Pewaukee

Resources Needed: Magazines, *Star Wars* memorabilia.

Evaluation Focus
⊠ Knowledge   ⊠ Attitude   ⊠ Problem Solving

Teacher's Notes (Things to change)

Junior High – Prevention and Control of Disease

Specific Topical Key: Lifestyle Assessment

Approximate Time: 50 minutes

Objective

The students will evaluate their past and present health practices and design positive changes for the future.

Activities

Using a lifestyle assessment tool provided by the teacher, students evaluate their current health practices in terms of the following: exercise, nutrition, weight control, tobacco, alcohol and other drugs, stress, and family history of disease.

Using the "Personal Wellness Planning" worksheet, students develop a personal health plan to implement positive changes for the future.

Source: *Wellness Kit*, Aid Association for Lutherans, Appleton, WI

Resources Needed: Lifestyle assessments such as *Operation Lifestyle* or *Healthstyle*.

Evaluation Focus
☒ Knowledge   ☒ Attitude   ☒ Problem Solving

Teacher's Notes (Things to change)

Junior High – Prevention and Control of Disease/Worksheet
Personal Wellness Planning

Where Do I Want to Go . . .

List some realistic goals in any dimension of personal wellness on the right side of the numbers.

_____	1.	_____
_____	2.	_____
_____	3.	_____
_____	4.	_____
_____	5.	_____
_____	6.	_____

What's Really Important . . .

Using the following four-point scale, give a value to each of your goals by writing the appropriate number in front of each.

1. Of *little* importance
2. Of *moderate* importance
3. Of *great* importance
4. Of *very great* importance

What's Really Important to Me . . .

Using your list above, write your top *three* goals in order of importance to *you*. Number 1 is most important, and so on.

1. _____

2. _____

3. _____

Making My Choice . . .

Select one of the top goals you would really like to begin to work on during the next two weeks. Write that goal in the box below. It should be clear enough so that when someone else sees it, he or she will understand what you have written.

```
┌─────────────────────────────────────────────────────────────┐
│ My goal:                                                      │
│                                                               │
│                                                               │
│                                                               │
│                                                               │
└─────────────────────────────────────────────────────────────┘
```

Junior High – Prevention and Control of Disease/Worksheet
Personal Wellness Planning

How Do I Get There...

Establish a plan for reaching your goal. Quickly think about the steps you must take and deadlines you must meet to reach your goal.

After you have organized your plan in your mind or on paper, share it with a friend or a member of your family. Ask the person to help you complete your plan, if that's possible. For example, you might ask the person to run with you or to plan a weekly menu.

This completes your wellness planning for this goal. You may wish to use the same process later for other goals to help you reach a higher level of health.

Senior High – Prevention and Control of Disease

Specific Topical Key: Health Promotion Outreach

Approximate Time: Ongoing

Objective

The students will design a plan aimed at disease prevention for themselves, their families, and the community.

Activities

Students and teacher are to plan a health promotion/disease prevention event, such as a walk, run, swim, cross-country ski race, or rope-jump to emphasize the importance of cardiovascular fitness. (**Note:** This is a long-range activity to be completed over a semester or more.)

In planning for the event, students and teacher should consider the following:
a) obtaining administrative and school board support;
b) planning an activity to raise money to cover expenses;
c) contacting local volunteer and professional organizations, such as the American Heart Association, American Lung Association, and public health and community agencies, to assist;
d) insuring local media coverage;
e) securing student, staff, and community volunteers to help run the event.

Evaluation Focus
☐ Knowledge ☒ Attitude ☒ Problem Solving

Teacher's Notes (Things to change)

Substance Use and Abuse

12

Focus
Student Objectives
Sample Lessons

Topics

Instructional units may be developed for these and other topics related to substance use and abuse: positive decision making, individual responsibility, substances beneficial to humankind, classification of substances and their effects on the body, formation of habits and their influence on health, use and misuse of tobacco, alcohol and other drugs, respect for oneself and others, setting goals, influence of advertising, peer influences, adult modeling.

Rationale

For students at all grade levels and ages, the primary objective of education is to prevent substance use and abuse. Programs should include educational strategies that stress individual responsibility for the daily decisions that affect health.

Cigarette smoking . . . is the single most important preventable cause of death.

Cigarette smoking is a crucial school health issue. Despite declines in all other groups, there has been an increase in female teenage smokers since 1974. Smoking has been identified as the cause of most cases of lung cancer and as a major factor which increases the risk of heart attack. Cigarette smoking, therefore, is the single most important preventable cause of death.

Drug and alcohol use and abuse are national problems. Both alcohol and drug misuse take a substantial toll in the form of preventable deaths, illnesses, and disabilities. This misuse also contributes to family problems and poor school and job performance, and it can lead to long-term chronic disease. Successful education is one way to confront problems related to substance use and abuse.

Life Goals

The individual
● adheres to medical recommendations when using drugs and medications;
● refrains from the abuse of potentially harmful and mood-modifying drugs;
● obeys laws and regulations regarding the use of controlled substances.

See also Personal Health, Mental and Emotional Health, Family Life Education, Consumer Health

Kindergarten

Recommended Minimum Time Allocation: six 15-minute periods/year

By the end of kindergarten, students will
1. name medicines and chemical substances that people use or abuse;
2. identify medicines commonly found in homes;
3. describe the different ways people take medicines;
4. explain reasons for consulting a responsible adult before using medicines or chemical substances.

Grade 1

Recommended Minimum Time Allocation: nine 25-minute periods/year

By the end of first grade, students will
1. describe what a medicine is;
2. give examples of how medicines may be helpful or harmful;
3. accurately identify medicines and chemical substances that they may come in contact with;
4. explain the risks involved in using unknown substances;
5. describe good risks and bad risks.

Grade 2

Recommended Minimum Time Allocation: nine 25-minute periods/year

By the end of second grade, students will
1. recognize names given to medicines and chemical substances;
2. describe the appropriate rules for taking medicines;
3. explain why people choose to avoid certain medicines or chemical substances;
4. describe how medicines and chemical substances affect the body.

Grade 3

Recommended Minimum Time Allocation: fifteen 25-minute periods/year

By the end of third grade, students will
1. discuss reasons for medicine and chemical substance use or nonuse;

2. explain the difference between use and abuse of drugs;
3. predict the effects of drug (including alcohol) use on physical, emotional, and social well-being;
4. list people and places who can provide help for medicine and chemical substance use problems;
5. recognize that some common products contain chemical substances such as caffeine, nicotine, and alcohol.

Grade 4

Recommended Minimum Time Allocation: fifteen 25-minute periods/year

By the end of fourth grade, students will
1. give reasons why people do and do not misuse and abuse specific drugs, including alcohol, tobacco, over-the-counter medicines, and prescription drugs;
2. recognize that there are alternatives to medicines and chemical substances that can enhance well-being;
3. describe the effects of alcohol, tobacco, and other drugs on organs of the body;
4. describe the behavioral effects of alcohol, tobacco, and other drugs;
5. tell why alcohol, tobacco, caffeine, over-the-counter medicines, and prescription drugs can be dangerous if misused.

Grade 5

Recommended Minimum Time Allocation: fifteen 50-minute periods/year

By the end of fifth grade, students will
1. apply the components of the decision-making process to drug nonuse or use situations;
2. appreciate the positive influences peers and adults can have on decisions concerning alcohol, tobacco, or other drug use;
3. demonstrate helpful strategies for dealing with social pressures to use drugs;
4. illustrate the impact use or abuse of alcohol, tobacco, and other drugs has on the individual, the family, and the community;
5. recognize the legal consequences of use, purchase, and possession of drugs.

Grade 6

Recommended Minimum Time Allocation: fifteen 50-minute periods/year

By the end of sixth grade, students will
1. value socially acceptable alternatives to tobacco, alcohol, and marijuana;

2. identify physical, mental, and social effects of tobacco, alcohol, and marijuana use;
3. develop personal plans to positively confront social pressures related to alcohol, tobacco, and other drug use;
4. identify people and organizations who can provide help with problems related to tobacco, alcohol, marijuana, and other drugs.

Grades 7-8-9, Junior High

Recommended Minimum Time Allocation: ten 50-minute periods/semester

By the end of ninth grade, students will
1. demonstrate stress management techniques that are alternatives to substance use or abuse;
2. describe situations which illustrate the interplay of personal, social, family, and environmental forces affecting the nonuse, use, or abuse of substances that modify behavior;
3. appreciate the possible negative consequences of the choice to use alcohol, tobacco, or other drugs;
4. explain why each individual is primarily responsible for his or her own decisions concerning the use or nonuse of alcohol, tobacco, and other drugs;
5. identify local resources, services, and support groups that are available for substance abuse treatment and control;
6. know about a wide variety of career choices and occupational opportunities available in the area of substance abuse prevention, intervention, and treatment.

Grades 10-11-12, Senior High

Recommended Minimum Time Allocation: ten 50-minute periods/semester

By the end of 12th grade, students will
1. recognize that decisions regarding nonuse, use, or abuse of tobacco, alcohol, and other drugs are affected by personal perceptions and have social implications;
2. assess how the nonuse, use, or abuse of alcohol, tobacco, and other drugs can result in immediate or gradual changes in health;
3. describe how to utilize programs and facilities designed to help individuals and families with tobacco, alcohol, and other drug problems;
4. recognize the risks involved with drug use, misuse, or abuse when operating or riding in recreation or transportation vehicles;
5. appreciate that everyone has the right to say "no" to the use of alcohol, tobacco, or other drugs;
6. analyze the effects of tobacco, alcohol, and other drugs during pregnancy.

Kindergarten – Substance Use and Abuse

Specific Topical Key: Ask Before Using

Approximate Time: 25 minutes

Objective

Students will give reasons for consulting a responsible adult before using medicines or chemical substances.

Students will explain why a substance cannot be identified by looking, tasting, or smelling.

Activities

The students are shown a piece of candy that looks like a pill. Ask them, "What is it?" "What else might it be?" "Can we tell what it is by looking at it or smelling it?" "What might happen if we swallowed it?"

Here are additional discussion questions.

- Can you determine if a pill is candy or medicine?
- What are medicines for?
- Should a person eat a pill that looks, smells, or tastes like candy without asking a qualified adult first? Why or why not?
- Who are some people you could ask before taking any medicines or something you are not sure about? (List on the chalkboard.)

Source: *Here's Looking at You, Two,* Comprehensive Health Education Foundation, Seattle, WA

Resources Needed: Piece of candy and a pill that look alike

Evaluation Focus
   ☒ Knowledge   ☒ Attitude   ☒ Problem Solving

Teacher's Notes (Things to change)

Grade 5 – Substance Use and Abuse

Specific Topical Key: Promote Non Smoking

Approximate Time: 50 minutes

Objective

Students will develop an information sheet describing the impact that use or abuse of tobacco has on the individual, the family, and the community.

Students will have a deterrent impact on the smoking habits of others.

Activities

In the course of a discussion, students are to make careful notes on the use of tobacco and its effects on the individual and society. An award system called "Smokebusters" is then used to encourage them to become actively involved in decreasing the number of smokers.

Each student must agree to present the information in his or her notes to a smoker they know. The smoker must sign a sheet indicating the student has indeed done this. On the same sheet, the smoker must also check *yes* or *no* in answer to the question, "Have you, after hearing the information presented, signed and attached to this sheet an 'intent to stop' statement?"

Each student who brings in a completed sheet signed by a smoker (in some cases, with a signed 'intent to stop' statement attached) gets a Smokebusters certificate, iron-on, or T-shirt.

This activity could be run in conjunction with the American Cancer Society's Great American Smoke-Out, or could be used as part of the American Lung Association's Students Teaching Students program.

I'M A SMOKEBUSTER

Grade 5 – Substance Use and Abuse *(continued)*

Source: Jon Hisgen, School District of Pewaukee

Resources Needed: Milwaukee Division of the American Cancer Society sample "Smokebusters" iron-on decal

Evaluation Focus

☒ Knowledge ☒ Attitude ☒ Problem Solving

Teacher's Notes (Things to change)

Junior High – Substance Use and Abuse

Specific Topical Key: Coping

Approximate Time: 50 minutes

Objective

The students will demonstrate stress management techniques that are alternatives to substance use or abuse.

The students will identify stressful situations in their lives.

Activities

In a class discussion, define "stressful feelings" (angry, anxious, embarrassed, hurt, lonely, sad, unsafe, unstable), and "stress/stressful situations" (circumstances in which we feel threatened by someone, something, or occurrences), and "coping" (dealing with a stressful feeling so that we feel better).

Explain that stress and dealing with stress are both natural parts of living. People use a variety of methods to cope with stress. Ask students for feelings they have when under stress and list these on the board.

Have students list three stressful situations in which they might feel sad, three in which they might feel angry, three in which they sometimes feel lonely, and three other stressful situations.

In these stressful situations, I might feel "sad."

1. _____

2. _____

3. _____

139

Junior High – Substance Use and Abuse *(continued)*

In these stressful situations, I might feel "angry!"

1. _____

2. _____

3. _____

In these stressful situations, I sometimes feel left out and lonely.

1. _____

2. _____

3. _____

In these other stressful situations, I might feel ....

1. _____

2. _____

3. _____

Facilitate an open-ended discussion using the following questions.
- Why do different people cope with their stressful feelings in different ways?
- If you have a coping behavior you don't like, what are some of your alternatives?
- If a friend has a coping behavior you don't like, what can you do?
- How can you better use your positive behaviors?
- When is it okay to feel bad? sad? frustrated? lonely?
- What might happen if you ignored your stressful feelings?
- How are drugs used in coping with stressful feelings?
- Why do some people use drugs for coping rather than other behaviors?

Have the students think of coping activities as emotional outlets and list four emotional outlets they could use for each of the following:
- when I am sad;
- when I am angry;
- when I am feeling lonely and left out;
- when I am worried.

See attached handout on "Emotional Outlets"

Source: *Here's Looking at You, Two,* Comprehensive Health Education Foundation, Seattle, WA

Evaluation Focus
    ☒ Knowledge   ☒ Attitude   ☒ Problem Solving

Teacher's Notes (Things to change)

Junior High – Substance Use and Abuse Handout

EMOTIONAL OUTLETS

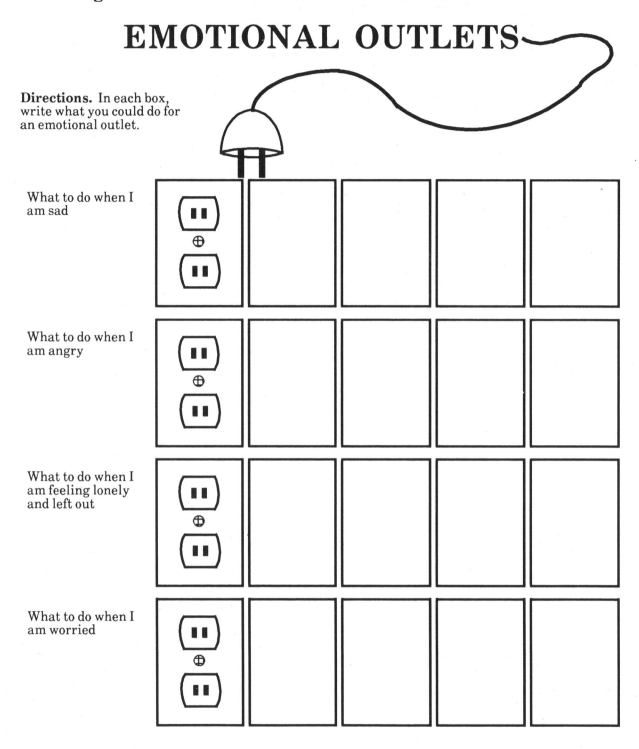

Directions. In each box, write what you could do for an emotional outlet.

What to do when I am sad

What to do when I am angry

What to do when I am feeling lonely and left out

What to do when I am worried

Senior High – Substance Use and Abuse

Specific Topical Key: Risk Profile

Approximate Time: 50 minutes

Objective

The students will recognize risks of drug use, misuse, or abuse when operating recreation or transportation vehicles.

Activities

Discuss what someone means when they say "that's a risky thing to do." Then ask what someone might mean by saying "you could gain a lot by doing that."

Define the terms "risk" and "gains" as the possible consequences of particular decisions.

Ask students to rate the level of risk-taking of a turtle—as either low, medium, or high. Explain that a turtle is well protected on top, can hide in its shell, but to go anywhere, has to stick out its neck. The point is that one takes some risks in order to gain something in return.

Tell students to develop a risk profile by listing and rating various behaviors under each of the headings below. The risk profile should include risk level (low, medium, high) and gain level (low, medium, high) for each behavior under each heading.

1) Driving
2) Recreational activities
3) Alcohol and other drug use
4) Peer relationships

Source: *Here's Looking at You, Two*, Comprehensive Health Education Foundation, Seattle, WA.

Evaluation Focus
☐ Knowledge   ☒ Attitude   ☒ Problem Solving

Teacher's Notes (Things to change)

Current and Future Issues

13

Teachers of Health Education

Outstanding teachers must actually deliver a quality program.

The most critical components of quality health instruction programs in our schools are teachers who are interested, prepared, and motivated to teach in the area of health education *with strong administrative support.* Two national studies in health education have found that in both the primary and secondary grades, school health education is either not provided at all or is assigned to teachers whose main interests and qualifications lie elsewhere. Quality health instruction at the local school district level does not just happen because a curriculum committee helps design a K–12 program. Outstanding teachers must actually deliver a quality program.

In Wisconsin, K–6 elementary classroom teachers are responsible for providing health instruction as part of their total educational programs. However, most elementary teachers in Wisconsin have not had more than one course in health education as part of their preservice professional preparation, and many may not have had any professional preparation in this area. Thus, special consideration must be given to the elementary classroom teacher; ongoing inservice activities aimed at improving teaching competence in health education, the use of new resources, and the establishment of two-way communication with others teaching the same units must be provided.

Since individual lifestyles are developed over a long period of time, elementary health instruction aimed at providing sound information and promoting positive attitudes and positive health behaviors has the potential to be the most important health instruction students receive during the school years.

At the secondary level, grades 7-12, health education taught as a discrete course must be conducted by a health teacher certified by the Department of Public Instruction. Just as at the elementary level, the quality of health instruction at the secondary level is determined by the interest, preparation, and enthusiasm of the health teacher. Even though secondary-level health teachers have completed a program qualifying them for certification in health education, the need for continuing professional development for these teachers cannot be over-emphasized. Participation in relevant inservice activities and professional conferences, along with specific graduate work in the area of health education, must be encouraged.

In addition to teaching, secondary-level health educators in many school districts are also looked upon as instructional leaders for the K–12 health education curriculum. Thus, school districts should give professionally prepared health teachers every opportunity to assist elementary and middle school staff as much as possible with provision of meaningful health instruction. Also, the entire K–12 health instruction program must have support and assistance from a wide range of human resources, as highlighted on the following chart.

Figure 4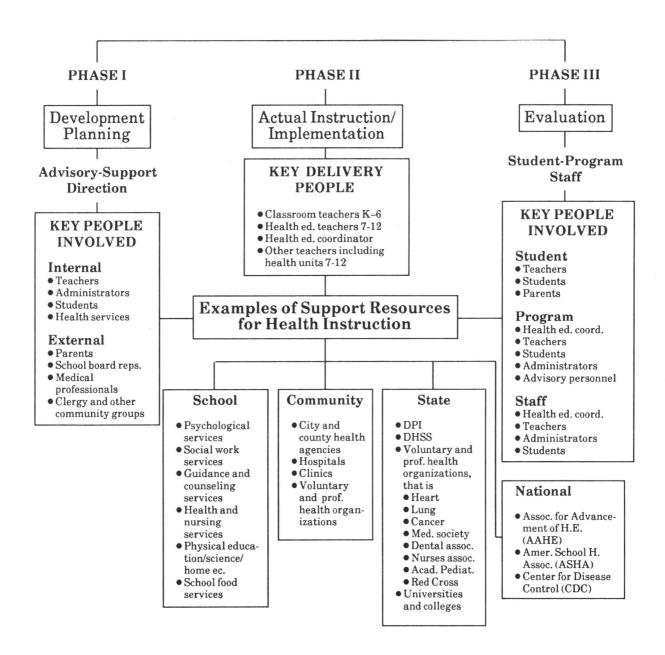

Organizational and Support Considerations for School Health Education

PHASE I

Development Planning

Advisory-Support Direction

KEY PEOPLE INVOLVED

Internal
- Teachers
- Administrators
- Students
- Health services

External
- Parents
- School board reps.
- Medical professionals
- Clergy and other community groups

PHASE II

Actual Instruction/ Implementation

KEY DELIVERY PEOPLE
- Classroom teachers K–6
- Health ed. teachers 7-12
- Health ed. coordinator
- Other teachers including health units 7-12

Examples of Support Resources for Health Instruction

School
- Psychological services
- Social work services
- Guidance and counseling services
- Health and nursing services
- Physical education/science/ home ec.
- School food services

Community
- City and county health agencies
- Hospitals
- Clinics
- Voluntary and prof. health organizations

State
- DPI
- DHSS
- Voluntary and prof. health organizations, that is
  - Heart
  - Lung
  - Cancer
  - Med. society
  - Dental assoc.
  - Nurses assoc.
  - Acad. Pediat.
  - Red Cross
- Universities and colleges

PHASE III

Evaluation

Student-Program Staff

KEY PEOPLE INVOLVED

Student
- Teachers
- Students
- Parents

Program
- Health ed. coord.
- Teachers
- Students
- Administrators
- Advisory personnel

Staff
- Health ed. coord.
- Teachers
- Administrators
- Students

National
- Assoc. for Advancement of H.E. (AAHE)
- Amer. School H. Assoc. (ASHA)
- Center for Disease Control (CDC)

147

Health Promotion for School Staff

. . . school health education and health promotion programs are economically irresistible.

During the past several years, private business and industry have discovered that healthy employes and those programs that promote their health can help reduce the trend toward ever-increasing health care costs, absenteeism, and decreased productivity. In 1982, the United States spent more than $320 billion for health care, with private and public employers paying at least half of these health care costs.

One of the more promising ways in which private business has confronted the problem of mounting health care costs and their impacts on the workplace and the economy has been to shift from a treatment-of-disease approach to the prevention of health problems through health promotion. In fact, there is available evidence to suggest that even modest health promotion programs can substantially reduce medical care costs in the workplace.

A new manual entitled *Wellness at the School Worksite* lists several compelling reasons for focusing health promotion efforts on the school as a unique worksite. The educational mission of the school as workplace seems an especially important reason. Carrying out that mission ought to involve active health promotion, influencing individuals, through education, to alter their health behaviors in positive ways. The following are other reasons for promoting health among all school staff.

● Schools are some of the largest employers in the country. Improving the health of such a substantial part of the work force would significantly affect national health care costs.

● Wellness/health promotion programs can improve school staff morale and productivity. That means not only better use of taxpayers' dollars, but also an improvement in the quality of education.

● Promoting wellness among school building staff has a built-in multiplier effect. Changing the health habits of a relative few will affect the health habits of a great many.

● Schools are everywhere; they provide geographic coverage of every state in the nation.

● Most schools already have fitness facilities, cafeterias, and trained health personnel, all excellent resources for health promotion.

● Schools have skilled professional staff trained in program design and management.

● Schools are potential community health promotion and wellness centers.

● Many schools and school systems have proven the effectiveness of "wellness at the school worksite" programs.

The manual also outlines a Wellness Cycle for both the school district and the individual. It includes screening, assessment, goal setting, group starter activities, feedback, and reassessment.

Besides the personal physical, emotional, and social benefits to all staff participating in a health promotion/wellness program in the school, documented financial benefits make such a program economically irresistible. The Dallas, Texas, Independent School District instituted a health promotion/wellness program in 1982, and after one year had saved nearly $500,000 in substitute teachers' pay. One of the most significant outcomes of this program was a 35-percent drop in absenteeism of participating teachers. In addition, the Dallas system reported the following:

- reduced smoking,
- decreased weight and body fat,
- decreased systolic and diastolic blood pressure,
- increased physical activity and exercise,
- increased use of balanced diet,
- decreased levels of anxiety and depression,
- increased sense of personal well-being,
- reduced health care claim costs,
- better morale,
- greater productivity,
- higher instructional quality due to improved teacher morale and more time on tasks with students.

A significant long-range goal of a health promotion/wellness program is to cut health care costs. School district investment in such a program is far more cost-effective than supporting the ever-increasing costs of treating disease and other preventable health problems. The immediate goal of health promotion is to improve staff morale and productivity in the school by fostering wellness. In addition, all school staff, "for better or for worse," are role models whose behavior influences the behavior of young people in their formative years. A health promotion program for staff, which may involve a relatively small number of employes, can have a positive influence on a great many students.

... all school staff, "for better or for worse," are role models ....

According to the findings of a Portland (Oregon) State University study, the existence of health promotion programs for staff is the number one predictor of successful health education programs in a school building. The number two predictor is the health-related behavior of the building principal.

If Wisconsin school staff responsible for health education believe that health instruction should be supported by the positive health lifestyles of faculty and other staff, then a health promotion/wellness program in the school setting is an idea whose time has come. For specific assistance in planning a health promotion/wellness program, interested schools can obtain a free copy of *Wellness at the School Worksite* by writing to:

Education Relations and Resources
Health Insurance Association of America
American Council of Life Insurance
1850 K Street, NW
Washington, DC 20006-2284
202-862-4082

This manual was developed in cooperation with the Association for the Advancement of Health Education.

Coordination of the School Health Education Program

One of the most difficult tasks for a local school district is the actual coordination and articulation of K-12 health instruction . . . .

. . . the health education coordinator must have a specific role description, approved by the board of education, in addition to professionally assigned time for coordination activities.

One of the most difficult tasks for a local school district is the actual coordination and articulation of K–12 health instruction and the use of support resources. The lack of coordination has been documented as a major weakness of school health education in two nationwide studies.

Since 1976, administrative rule for Wisconsin state statute 121.02 (1) (l) has required local school districts to designate a professional staff member as coordinator of health education. The purpose of this is to assure that one person has primary responsibility for providing the motivation and leadership necessary for the development, implementation, and evaluation of a local K–12 school health instruction program. It is critical that the school board and district administration give this person legitimate authority, responsibility, and time to exercise the instructional leadership necessary to actually coordinate and articulate the program. Logically, this individual should have professional preparation in health education and high interest in assuming the role of district coordinator.

To be successful, the health education coordinator must have a specific role description, approved by the board of education, in addition to assigned professional time for coordination activities.

A sample role description can be found in Appendix A.

Obviously, one individual in a school district cannot coordinate a program without the assistance and cooperation of other interested staff. It is recommended that the coordinator identify a health education contact person in each school building to work as part of a districtwide health education coordinating team. Each building contact person would become the leader for health education initiatives within that specific school. In addition, each individual should be given legitimate authority by the principal to represent all teaching staff involved in health instruction at the building level.

The coordinating team members and health education coordinator should meet frequently during the school year to discuss problems, solutions, new ideas and teaching strategies, and new resources useful for program development, implementation, and evaluation. In addition, team members should have frequent opportunities to participate in continuing professional staff development in health education. As these staff members gain new skills and knowledge, they can conduct ongoing health education inservice programs for other staff members in each school building.

The health education coordinator and the members of the coordinating team can actually institutionalize K–12 health instruction at the local school district level. However, the keys to the success of the coordinating team are their interest, their motivation, and the legitimacy of the role and function given to that team by the district administrative staff and the local board of education.

In addition to coordination, the following significant management functions should be considered at the local district level.

Advocacy

Health education requires advocacy. Good health education programs do not just happen. Someone makes them happen. Those who believe comprehensive health education can help people live healthier, more productive lives must make that belief known to educational policymakers at all levels.

Good health education programs do not just happen.

Clearinghouse

Vital to the management of a comprehensive school health education program are clearinghouse functions. Health education staff should constantly seek visibility for the program and should use available resources, especially those in the community. The purpose of the clearinghouse function is to promote awareness of, to review, and to disseminate information about the availability of quality health education resources and resource needs. Resources include ideas, people, methods, materials, facilities, programs, research projects, and funding sources.

Evaluation

The purpose of evaluation is to gather information about effectiveness and efficiency that can be used to make decisions about programs. Evaluation can provide information about program efforts to policymakers, advocacy groups, and resource people. It may be used to generate continuing support for programs or to show a need for new efforts. Evaluation should help staff to discover practical ways to improve their efforts.

Evaluation should help staff to discover practical ways to improve their efforts.

Innovation

Innovation is important in health education because the field is changing rapidly. There are innovations that provide solutions to particular problems and that outline new and promising approaches to the health education curriculum. It is usually best to pilot each innovation to evaluate its utility and see if it can be practically implemented within the existing program.

Teachers should be encouraged to plan and implement new teaching strategies and use new resources that support the program's goals and objectives. When innovative ideas and resources are successful or useful, they should be shared with other teaching staff.

The five areas addressed here, coordination, advocacy, clearinghouse, evaluation, and innovation, are described in much more detail in a publication entitled *Comprehensive Health Education Management Model.*

This management model was developed for the U.S. Department of Health and Human Services, Bureau of Health Education, Center for Disease Control, by the Florida Department of Education. An adaptation for local district management of the model presented in this document is available from the Department of Public Instruction's health education supervisor. See Appendix B.

Resources for Health Instruction

... when schools assume the responsibility for planning, implementing, and evaluating their health instruction programs, they must apply sound principles and criteria in the selection and use of resource materials.

School health instruction materials are produced by many volunteer, professional, and commercial organizations. While the quality of such materials varies widely, many of them are useful and inexpensive. However, the proliferation of such materials and the enthusiasm with which they are promoted to schools frequently encourages fragmentation of an existing curriculum and the use of diverse and unrelated materials as a substitute for a developmental, sequential, comprehensive, and balanced health instruction program. These materials, when used, should be integrated within the instructional program. In addition, when schools assume the responsibility for planning, implementing, and evaluating their health instruction programs, they must apply sound principles and criteria in the selection and use of resource materials.

To assist school districts with this task, this guide has identified sources of health information and materials at the national, state, regional, and local levels. This listing can be found in Appendix B.

In addition to the resource list, the guide includes an article entitled "Practical Principles in the Effective Use of Print Materials" (Appendix C). This article is reprinted with permission of the copyright owner from a book entitled *Education-for-Health: The Selective Guide*, published by the National Center for Health Education. The article, written by Dr. Nina Ridenour, outlines specific principles and criteria to guide those selecting and using health education resources. Five basic qualities to look for when assessing educational materials are discussed in the article. These qualities are

- substance,
- validity,
- balance,
- authority,
- integrity.

While the article focuses primarily on print materials, the criteria given can certainly be applied when selecting human and audiovisual resources as well. In addition to the five qualities above, creativity and motivational value are also extremely important.

Finally, additional guidance in selection of resources, including textbooks, can be found in *A Guide for Curriculum Planning in Reading*, in the section on "Selecting Instructional Materials."

One of the most sensitive topics which school districts must consider when designing their comprehensive health education program is instruction about human sexuality. The position taken by the Department of Public Instruction is that *the primary responsibility for education about sexuality as one area of total human growth and development rests with the parents, guardians, or other persons responsible for minor-aged children.* However, the school certainly has an opportunity to supplement and complement those standards and programs established at home and within the community.

Ultimately, the decision as to whether or not an instructional program about human sexuality is to be introduced into the schools is a matter for the school board to determine at the local district level. The DPI makes the following recommendations to school boards considering such programs.

... focus on the need for positive interpersonal relationships within the family. ...

● Student participation in instruction about human sexuality should be voluntary and subject to parental consent.

● Local school boards must seek community support from parents, guardians, clergy, physicians, other health professionals, and interested citizens to define the role of the community's schools in providing instruction about human sexuality.

● A major goal of the school program should be to give youth the opportunity to understand and appreciate the value of family life.

● Teachers assigned the responsibility for including instruction about human sexuality must

— have the interest, motivation, preparation, and confidence necessary to provide meaningful instruction to students;

— have earned the trust and confidence of the school administration, parents, and the students whom they will instruct;

— be extremely careful in the selection and use of supplementary resources that support the basic instructional program;

— establish realistic limits concerning the scope of the instructional program;

— protect and respect student and family privacy in all class activities and assignments;

— preview audiovisual and print materials with an advisory group before using them with students.

In addition to the above, it is recommended that school districts make every effort to assure that any program which includes the study of human sexuality *emphasize the strengthening of the family unit.* Also, such a program should focus on the need for positive interpersonal relationships within the family, and promote the concept that adults must recognize and assume their responsibilities for rearing children.

For additional assistance in planning instruction about human sexuality, school districts should contact the CESA human growth and development coordinators in their areas of the state. See Appendix B.

Equity in Health Education

A quality health education program eliminates both personal and professional biases.

The state and the nation recognize the differences in the experiences of women and of men, of all races, colors, and ethnic groups, and of people of varied physical and mental abilities. These differences often result in the sorting, grouping, and tracking of minority, female, and disabled students into stereotyped patterns that prevent them from exploring all options and opportunities according to their individual talents and interests. The cost of bias to academic achievement, psychological and physical development, careers, and family relationships is significant. Each student should have the opportunity to see his or her own place in a health education curriculum.

To that end, this guide recommends the inclusion of all groups in a health education curriculum and in teaching resources. A quality health education program eliminates both personal and professional biases.

Every effort must be made to eliminate the following forms of bias.

Invisibility: underrepresentation of certain groups, which can imply that these groups are of less value, importance, and significance.

Stereotyping: assigning only traditional and rigid roles or attributes to a group, thus limiting the abilities and potential of that group; denying students a knowledge of the diversity and complexity of, and variations among, any group of individuals.

Imbalance/selectivity: presenting only one interpretation of an issue, situation, or group; distorting reality and ignoring complex and differing viewpoints through selective presentation of materials.

Unreality: presenting an unrealistic portrayal of this country's history and contemporary life experience.

Fragmentation/isolation: separating issues related to minorities and women from the main body of the text.

Linguistic bias: excluding the roles and importance of females by constant use of the generic *he* and sex-biased words.

Health education curriculum committees are urged to actively emphasize the value of all persons by including the contributions, images, and experiences of all groups in curricular objectives and classroom activities.

154

Strengthening Reading Skills

The Directed Reading Thinking Activity (DRTA) is a general model for teaching subject-area reading; it incorporates much of the appropriate knowledge and recent research regarding reading comprehension instruction. The DRTA is described in detail in the Department of Public Instruction *Guide to Curriculum Planning in Reading,* which should be consulted by those wishing a more complete description of the activity. The DRTA model provides an instructional framework for integrating specific reading strategies or processes into the health education content while encouraging development of critical reading and thinking skills that can be applied to all subject areas.

The DRTA involves five stages: preparation for reading, setting a purpose, guided silent reading, discussion, rereading plus reflection, and extension activities. The following sections will describe each of these, offering instruction and application suggestions for teachers of health education.

Preparation for Reading

Before giving a reading assignment, examine the reading selection or text to determine the features that would help student comprehension and to identify both unfamiliar vocabulary and concepts that might be difficult for students. Next, assess students' experiential backgrounds to decide whether they have the necessary concepts and vocabulary knowledge to extract a satisfactory level of meaning from the text. If this background is insufficient, it will be necessary to decide how best to help students acquire this information before they read the selection. Vocabulary instruction research seems to indicate that focusing on concepts and meanings in familiar contexts is more profitable than rote learning of new words in isolation. Thus, one should teach unfamiliar vocabulary essential to understanding text material in rich contextual settings which are relevant and interesting before and during reading.

The following are some specific suggestions for preparing students for reading in health texts or other health-related materials.

● Assess and expand the students' background knowledge and experience as related to the text or assignment by

   — questioning students directly to find out what they know or believe they know;

   — noting misconceptions and offering information to provide adequate background for comprehension;

   — arousing interest and helping students become aware of the relevance of text material to their daily lives.

- Introduce necessary vocabulary and fundamental concepts by
    - brainstorming with students about the general meanings of new words;
    - guiding students to more specific meanings of new words in the assigned text;
    - analyzing the structure of the new words to aid recognition (roots, prefixes, suffixes);
    - developing links between vocabulary and larger concepts.

Setting a Purpose

The more thoroughly students are prepared to identify text features and to set purpose, the more likely they are to comprehend.

Through this procedure, students begin to identify a purpose for their reading. Focus students' attention on important concepts contained in the text. For example, if you want students to identify the benefits of a fitness program, point out that a list of such benefits may be derived from the reading. If human anatomy or exact physical systems terminology is desired, make that clear, so that students have some sense of what aspects of the text material to focus upon.

Guided Silent Reading

Once they have reading purposes clearly in mind, students are ready to read the assigned material silently. To promote effective silent reading, encourage students to create questions which they can refer to as they read.

Discussion, Rereading, and Reflection

Following purposeful silent reading, guide students in the discussion of the specific reading. Provide them an opportunity to talk about the content in relation to their purposes for reading it. They should discuss whether the information acquired was sufficient to answer their questions and fulfill expectations.

Critical Thinking

During discussion, ask questions requiring students to go beyond the specific details and think critically about the overall concepts and longer messages in the text. Ask them to reread sections to find support for their interpretations or to identify inconsistencies in the author's reasoning. Rereading can be done either aloud or silently, but should always have a definite purpose.

Following are specific activities involving discussion, reading, and reflections:
- discussing answers to prereading questions, confirming and verifying answers;

- interpreting information from reading by drawing conclusions, making inferences, generalizing, and identifying interrelationships;
- evaluating information by making judgments, determining intent, and considering the overall significance of the information;
- reflecting upon information by applying it to current, real-life situations;
- identifying topics for further analysis, discussion, and perhaps writing.

Extension Activities

Extension activities help students expand upon information gained from the reading. They provide students with opportunities to incorporate new ideas and information into their background understandings.

Strengthening Writing Skills

Writing and Learning

Because writing and learning are such similar processes, teachers who include writing as a learning activity in their classrooms find that students understand and retain knowledge better. Both writing and learning require active attempts to make meaning out of experience and information. Both require planning ahead and reviewing; both are focused on making connections between prior knowledge and new information. Writing has the special advantage of making a student's thought processes visible and available in a permanent form. This permanent record is useful in the rehearsing and reviewing process necessary for long-term learning.

Writing has the special advantage of making a student's thought processes visible and available in a permanent form.

It is important that teachers who use writing to enhance learning in a specific content area realize that they need not take on all the burdens of the English teacher. The following guidelines for assignments and evaluation may help explain how writing can enhance content-area learning.
- Frequent short writing assignments are more helpful than one long assignment.
- Not all writing has to be evaluated. Students need to write far more material than any teacher can grade if writing is to improve their learning.
- There is a variety of ways to give students helpful feedback on their writing. Feedback given on outlines and drafts improves students' writing more than extensive correcting or comments on already completed assignments.
- Student writing can provide information on the success of instruction. Having students write short summary paragraphs at the ends of lessons gives feedback on their comprehension of the material.

Sample Writing Assignments

The following are offered as appropriate writing activities within a health instruction program.

Writing Directions. When instruction focuses on how a particular procedure is done or on describing a particular process, have students write directions for someone unfamiliar with the process (*not* for the teacher). Students must first understand the process and be able to explain it in their own words before they can explain it to someone else. Choosing an audience other than the teacher emphasizes the need to be clear and inclusive, since the audience has no prior understanding of the process.

Defining Terms. When instruction focuses on learning new vocabulary for concepts and objects, have students write definitions for these terms in their own words. Emphasize making connections to objects and concepts with which students are already familiar.

Performance Critique. When students are learning to perform a skill and process, like CPR, have them critique their own performance in writing. When they do this, students review their behavior, spot any errors, retrieve their last correct behavior, and determine alternative behavior. This teaches self-monitoring strategies.

News Features/Editorials. Ask students to write articles for a local paper on health-related topics. Giving information on a topic and supplying persuasive reasons for certain behaviors will not only increase each student's understanding of the material, but also help him or her learn what motivates people to change their behaviors.

Complete information on writing and learning is available in *A Guide to Curriculum Planning in Language Arts*.

Computers in Health Education

A fundamental need in an information-age society is for children to learn to handle information, to solve problems, to communicate with people, and to understand the changes that are taking place in their society.

Greater use of electronic educational tools can significantly increase the effectiveness of education. Such tools can take students beyond traditional health education to a future-oriented curriculum that offers problem-solving activities not previously available.

The computer's potential as an effective instructional tool for a variety of applications has been demonstrated. Computers may be used to manage the instructional setting, particularly as aids in test scoring, grading, and record keeping. Computer software can help teachers diagnose areas of weakness in, and suggest appropriate assignments for, their students. Districts may also look to the computer for curriculum maintenance; as district goals and objectives for students change over time, the computer allows additions to, deletions from, and modifications of curriculum and resource data to be made with ease.

A number of school administrative functions, some of which directly influence decisions made for the health instruction program, may also be handled by the computer. These include student records management, planning and budgeting applications, and information systems.

In computer-aided learning, computer programs become effective instructional tools used in much the same way other media resources are used.

Well-developed computer software can add dynamic and interactive versatility to the learning process. The following applications make the computer an instructional tool for health education.

. . . computer programs become effective instructional tools used in much the same way other media resources are used.

Drill and practice programs review and reinforce concepts or skills already taught.

Tutorial programs introduce and explain concepts and facts; they may also provide initial exposure to materials.

Simulation programs are designed to model real-world environments with which students can investigate areas of fitness, nutrition, stress management, ecology, weight control, substance use, and so on. Simulations allow students to make decisions and interact in situations that are often historical or too complex, expensive, dangerous, or distant to be brought into the classroom.

Discovery computer programs are used to develop cognitive problem-solving abilities in specific topic areas such as alcohol and other drug abuse, consumerism, disease prevention, accident prevention, and others.

Instructional games are designed to hold a user's attention and interest while teaching logical thinking or making practice less tedious.

Word processing involves use of the computer and specialty software which supports the writing, editing, formatting, and printing of reports and other written documents.

Data bases can be created using the computer's ability to collect, organize, retrieve, sort, display, and print data of all kinds.

Spreadsheets are business or scientific worksheets that may be simulated using the computer and specialized software. Data are entered into "cells" in the electronic worksheet and can be calculated automatically by the spreadsheet program.

Telecommunications involves use of the computer and communications software to input, transmit, sort, receive, and display information from various sources.

Specific information concerning the use of computers in education is available from the DPI supervisor, microcomputers and instructional technology, Division for Library Services.

For more information on the use of computers and software in health education, contact the Association for the Advancement of Health Education. In addition, the National Health Information Clearinghouse has published a listing of *Health Promotion Software*. See Appendix B for information on both organizations.

Teaching Strategies for Health Education*

Effective health teaching depends greatly upon the instructor's ability to motivate students . . . .

How health is taught is just as important as *what* is taught. The teacher must give special attention to the strategies and methods used to ensure that techniques are varied and provide continuity and progressive learning for all students. Students develop health understandings, habits, skills, and attitudes by experiencing a wide variety of activities. Effective health teaching depends greatly upon the instructor's ability to motivate students to make positive health choices.

Those teachers who show interest, preparation, and enthusiasm will capture the students' attention, arouse their interest, and probably be most successful in influencing their understandings and attitudes and in helping them to perceive the goal of high-level wellness as worthwhile.

Teaching strategies in health instruction, as in any other area of teaching, should relate directly to the teacher's goals and objectives for students. In health instruction, the goals of acquiring information, developing concepts, learning skills, becoming aware of values, and developing inquiry strategies are all important and necessary. An emphasis on finding personal meaning and on involvement will help students to internalize the concepts, skills, and information presented.

Therefore, the teaching strategies most necessary to the development of positive health behaviors in students are, perhaps, those that help them learn problem-solving and decision-making skills. Developing a means of inquiry and the ability to think critically is essential if each student is to assume responsibility for the lifelong task of maintaining personal well-being.

*Adapted from *Guidelines for Improving School Health Education K–12,* Ohio Department of Education.

Decision Making

Young people need practice with decision making, for it brings into play many of the elements of critical thinking. Among these are the abilities to observe, listen, and read to acquire information; to classify information into specific categories; to compare and contrast known facts; and to interpret or analyze information acquired before a judgment is made as to the best course of action.

Students need to be able to process specific health concepts and facts before deciding what course of action to take and whether to change their behaviors or attitudes. To make responsible decisions, students need help with

- identifying the problem (classifying, categorizing),
- acquiring information (observing, listening, questioning),
- checking out options (comparing, contrasting),
- checking reasonableness of options (analyzing, interpreting),
- selecting appropriate solution (making judgments, predicting),
- applying conclusions (accepting consequences).

If students possess the skills to make intelligent decisions, they will be equipped to make intelligent judgments about most health-related questions and problems.

Young people need practice with decision-making . . . .

Problem Solving

A teacher acquainted with problem-solving skills can also help students practice these skills when they make decisions about personal, family or public health. The following logical sequence for problem solving was first outlined by John Dewey many years ago.

- Identify the problem.
- Establish the facts.
- Formulate hypotheses.
- Test hypotheses.
- Evaluate results.

It is especially important to help students learn to make decisions affecting their well-being, not out of habit or in response to an advertisement, but using an intellectual and critical thinking approach. Critical thinking involves both deductive or analytical thought (principle to facts) and inductive or synthetic thought (facts to principle). Most decisions in life are made using a combination of the two; therefore, teachers must directly teach and offer practice in critical thinking in the schools.

. . . help students learn to make decisions affecting their well-being, not out of habit or in response to an advertisement, but using an intellectual and critical thinking approach.

Health Careers in Wisconsin

14

Career Development
Wisconsin Career Information System
Health Careers and Occupations

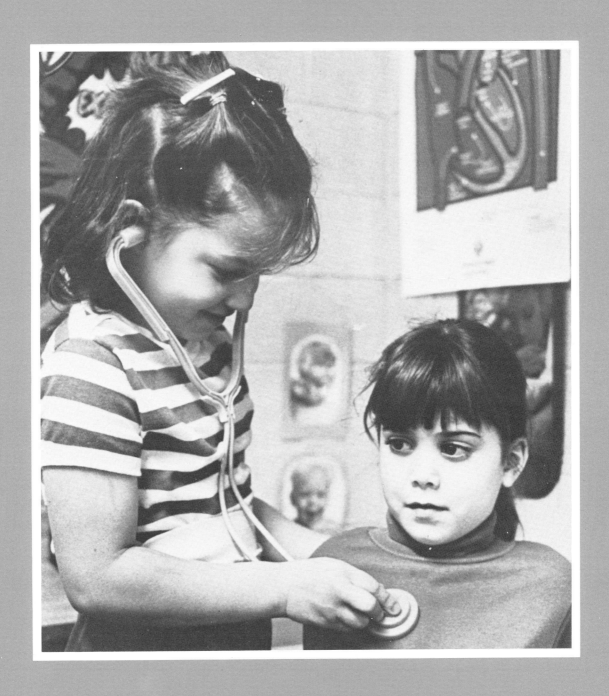

Career Development

This curriculum guide includes proposed objectives, within the ten major content areas, for increasing student knowledge of career choices and occupational opportunities available in the health field. This section stresses the importance of career development as it relates to a broad list of health-related careers and occupations. It is recommended that the planners of junior and senior high school health education courses seriously consider including instruction about a wide range of health careers and occupations in the basic health instructional program.

Activities should help students become more aware of and explore health occupations.

Career development is a continuous process which identifies various stages of change a person may experience throughout his or her lifetime. These stages are affected by individual goals, skills, and values as they interrelate with the various career options and alternatives each individual pursues. Obviously, teachers must be able to recognize various levels of maturity and readiness in students in order to help them identify personal strengths, abilities to work with others, and information on the world of work, the variety of choices available, and the requirements of and rewards offered by relevant health occupations. Activities should help students become more aware of and explore health occupations.

Wisconsin Career Information System

The following list of health careers and occupations has been compiled by the Wisconsin Career Information System (WCIS) specifically for this curriculum guide. The occupations are all health related, and are listed under the ten major content areas recommended as basic components of a comprehensive school health education program.

The Wisconsin Career Information System has been in operation since 1975 and is an attempt to deliver a comprehensive career counseling program to many different groups throughout the state. WCIS provides an array of pre-occupational search activities and exercises to help individuals clarify their goals and interests. Then, a variety of search modes help users match these goals and interests with occupations. There are main frame and microcomputer search programs and printed search materials.

After potential occupations are identified, users receive extensive information about the occupations they have selected. Again, there is both printed and computer access to this information. It includes descriptions of worker tasks, methods of job entry, Wisconsin and national outlook data and predictions, worker likes and dislikes, and references to other sources of information.

The availability of education information makes WCIS even more useful. The system lists required education and training programs for each occupation and Wisconsin schools offering such programs. National college information is also included. In addition, users may read about technologies that are changing the American workplace and how these changes may affect the occupations in which they are interested and their occupational choices.

Many Wisconsin school districts are subscribers to the WCIS program. Health teachers should contact school counseling staff to see if their school districts are participants in this system. Teachers in districts that do not participate may obtain information on WCIS by writing:

Wisconsin Career Information System
1078 Educational Services Unit I
1025 West Johnson Street
Madison, Wisconsin 53706
Telephone: 608/263-2725

The following list of health-related occupations identified by WCIS should suggest to health teachers a wide range of opportunities to provide instruction on health careers and occupations. Some occupations are appropriately included in more than one category. For example, psychiatrists are listed under mental and emotional health as well as personal health. Some occupations that are not primarily health care occupations are included. For example, public relations managers are listed because hospital public relations is a major specialty within that communications field. Other examples are food technologists and industrial hygienists. These workers are concerned with maintaining health standards, but are not directly involved in the treatment of disease.

Health Careers and Occupations

Accident Prevention and Safety

WCIS #

1131	Judicial, public safety, and corrections administrators
1473B	Industrial safety inspectors
1473C	Driver's license examiners
3690F	Emergency medical technicians
5132B	Police officers
5142A	Crossing guards
5144A	Guards
5123A	Firefighters

Community Health

Consumer Health

Environmental Health

Family Life Education

Mental and Emotional Health

Nutrition

Personal Health

2359A	Teachers, special education
2359B	Teachers for the blind
2390A	Physical education teachers
2400B	Vocational rehabilitation counselors
2610A	Family practitioners
2610B	Surgeons
2610C	Pathologists
2610D	Psychiatrists
2610E	Osteopaths
2620A	Dentists
2810A	Optometrists
2830A	Podiatrists
2890A	Chiropractors
2910A	Registered nurses
2910B	Nurse practitioners
2910C	Nurse anesthetists
3020A	Dietitians
3031A	Respiratory therapists
3032B	Occupational therapists
3033A	Physical therapists
3034A	Speech and language clinicians
3040A	Physician's assistants
3290B	Interpreters for the deaf
3630A	Dental hygienists
3660A	Licensed practical nurses
3690F	Emergency medical technicians
3690H	Dialysis technicians
5232A	Dental assistants
5233A	Podiatric assistants
5233B	Occupational therapy assistants
5236A	Home health aides
5236B	Psychiatric aides
5236C	Nurses' aides
6864A	Opticians

Prevention and Control of Disease

WCIS #

1855A	Cancer researchers
2610A	Family practitioners
2610C	Pathologists
2620A	Dentists
3020A	Dietitians
3630A	Dental hygienists
3690D	Medical laboratory assistants
5246A	Pest control workers

Substance Use and Abuse

WCIS #

2032D	Alcohol and drug abuse counselors
2610A	Family practitioners
3010A	Pharmacists
3020A	Dietitians
4237A	Chemical and drug sales associates

The next two categories were added by WCIS and include occupations which were not listed under the other ten areas. Examples include medical and scientific illustrators and veterinarians.

Medical/Health
Products/Research/Technologies

WCIS #

1693B	Biomedical engineers
1855B	Genetic/biotechnical engineers
1843	Physicists
1854	Biological scientists
1854A	Microbiologists
3620A	Medical technologists
3620B	Ultrasound technologists
3640A	Medical records technicians
3650A	Radiologic technologists
3690A	Prosthetists/orthotists
3690B	Electrocardiograph technicians
3690C	Electroencephalograph technicians
3690D	Medical laboratory assistants
3690G	Operating room technicians
3690H	Dialysis technicians

Other Health-related Fields

WCIS #

2700A	Veterinarians
3250B	Medical and scientific illustrators
3970A	Computer programmers
3970B	Scientific and engineering programmers
3980A	Technical writers
4236	Technical sales workers: medical and dental equipment and supplies
4511A	Supervisors: office occupations
4622B	Medical secretaries

4630A	General office clerks
4642A	Hospital admitting clerks
4664	Order clerks
4696A	File clerks
4715	Billing clerks
4732A	Telephone operators
4744A	Mail clerks
4754A	Medical central supply clerks
4793A	Word processor operators
5624A	Veterinary technicians
6171C	Electromedical equipment repairers

Appendixes 15

Role Description for a Health Education Coordinator

The following outline identifies specific duties, knowledge, and abilities; it could be used to design a specific role description for a district health education coordinator.

Specific Duties

- Emphasize the importance of and gain support for school health education within the school and community.
- Assist with the development of a needs assessment for K–12 health instruction.
- Help determine program needs and priorities, taking into consideration the needs assessment, the status of existing instruction, and community expectations.
- Provide leadership in identifying and upgrading content to be covered in the local K–12 curriculum.
- Understand and interpret state laws mandating school health education and curriculum guidelines developed by the Department of Public Instruction.
- Act as the catalyst for coordination and articulation of K–12 health instruction with the district health education coordinating team.
- Assist with the design of inservice workshops for administrators and teachers to provide information, review new resources, explore new teaching strategies, and improve communication among all involved publics.
- Provide leadership necessary to design and implement health promotion and wellness activities for school staff.
- Establish two-way communication with organizational and support services within the school, community, and state and involve such services in the school program. This would include, but not be limited to, pupil services staff, health services staff, physicians, health agencies, volunteer organizations, hospitals, universities and colleges, Wisconsin Division of Health staff, and Wisconsin Department of Public Instruction health staff.
- Provide assistance with designing evaluation components of the instructional program.
- Assist with the identification, evaluation, and selection of relevant resources to support the instructional program.

Knowledge of

- the total health principle of balanced physical, emotional, social, and intellectual growth and development
- the many topical areas included in health instruction and their relationship to total health
- teaching techniques as they apply to specific topical areas and total health
- teaching and motivational strategies and their applications at various grade levels and for students with varying degrees of maturity
- curriculum development and implementation for school health education
- current resource materials available and how they relate to total health and can be used in health instruction
- the principles, practices, and legal framework of school administration and district organization
- strategies and motivational techniques used to involve staff in health promotion and wellness activities

Skills

Ability to

- establish and maintain effective, cooperative relationships with fellow employees, administrative staff, school board representatives, supportive organizations, and the general public
- speak and communicate effectively before large and small groups
- write on an advanced professional level
- present ideas in a persuasive manner
- lead and participate in group discussions
- critique new programs, ideas, and techniques for possible use in schools
- demonstrate leadership and professional preparation in school health education

Resources/National

There are multitudinous resources available to those who teach health education. The following outline is not all-inclusive but does identify selected sources of health information and materials.

National Health Information Clearinghouse
P.O. Box 1133, Washington, DC 20013-1133
(800) 336-4797 [toll free]

The National Health Information Clearinghouse (NHIC), part of the Office of Disease Prevention and Health Promotion, United States Public Health Service, is a central source of information and referrals for health questions.

The NHIC has identified many groups and organizations that provide health information to the public. When a person contacts the NHIC with a question, the Information Services staff determines which of these resources can best provide an answer. An NHIC staff member contacts the resource, which responds directly to the questioner. The NHIC staff can only provide health information; they cannot give medical advice, diagnose, or recommend treatment.

In August of 1984, the NHIC published the following adapted list of "Selected Federal Health Information Clearinghouses and Information Centers."

The federal government operates a number of clearinghouses and information centers, most of which focus on a single topic, such as drug abuse or high blood pressure. Their services vary but may include publications, referrals, or answers to consumer inquiries. The information resources listed below are arranged in alphabetical order by key word, which is the term or terms appearing in **bold type.**

National Clearinghouse for **Alcohol** Information, P.O. Box 2345, Rockville, MD 20852; (301) 468-2600. Gathers and disseminates current information on alcohol-related subjects. Responds to requests from the public as well as from health professionals. Distributes a variety of publications on alcohol abuse.

Cancer Information Clearinghouse, National Cancer Institute, Office of Cancer Communications, Building 31, Room 10A-18, 9000 Rockville Pike, Bethesda, MD 20205; (301) 496-4070. Collects information on public and patient cancer education materials and disseminates it to organizations and health care professionals.

Clearinghouse on **Child Abuse and Neglect** Information, P.O. Box 1182, Washington, DC 20013; (301) 251-5157. Collects, processes, and disseminates information on child abuse and neglect. Responds to requests from the general public and professionals.

Consumer Information Center, Pueblo, CO 81009. Distributes consumer publications on topics such as children, food and nutrition, health, exercise, and weight control. The *Consumer Information Catalog* is available free from the center and must be used to identify publications being requested.

National Clearinghouse for **Drug Abuse** Information, P.O. Box 416, Kensington, MD 20795; (301) 443-6500. Collects and disseminates information on drug abuse. Produces informational materials on drugs, drug abuse, and prevention. Provides information to both consumers and health professionals.

Environmental Protection Agency, Public Information Center, Room PM 211-B, 401 M Street SW, Washington, DC 20460; (202) 829-3535. Public information materials on such topics as hazardous wastes, the school asbestos project, air and water pollution, pesticides, and drinking water are available. Offers information on the agency and its programs and activities.

Food and Drug Administration, Office of Consumer Affairs, 5600 Fishers Lane, Rockville, MD 20857; (301) 443-3170. Answers consumer inquiries and serves as a clearinghouse for its consumer publications.

National Information Center for **Handicapped Children and Youth,** P.O. Box 1492, Washington, DC 20013. Helps parents of handicapped children, disabled adults, and professionals locate services for the handicapped and information on disabling conditions.

Center for **Health Promotion and Education,** Centers for Disease Control, Building 1 South, Room SSB249, 1600 Clifton Road NE., Atlanta, GA 30333; (404) 329-3492; (404) 329-3698. Provides leadership and program direction for the prevention of disease, disability, premature death, and undesirable and unnecessary health problems through health education. Formerly called the Bureau of Health Education.

High Blood Pressure Information Center, 120/80, National Institutes of Health, Bethesda, MD 20205; (301) 496-1809. Provides information on the detection, diagnosis, and management of high blood pressure to consumers and health professionals.

National **Highway Traffic Safety** Administration, NTS-11, U.S. Department of Transportation, 400 7th Street SW., Washington, DC 20590; (202) 426-9294; Auto Hotline: (800) 424-9393; (202) 426-0123 (in DC). Works to reduce highway traffic deaths and injuries. Publishes a variety of safety information brochures, conducts health promotion and risk reduction public education programs that promote the use of safety belts and child safety seats, and informs the public of the hazards of drunk driving. Maintains a toll-free hotline for consumer complaints on auto safety and child safety seats and requests for information on recalls.

National **Injury** Information Clearinghouse, 5401 Westbard Avenue, Room 625, Washington, DC 20207; (301) 492-6424. Collects and disseminates injury data and information relating to the causes and prevention of death, injury, and illness associated with consumer products. Requests of a general nature are referred to the Consumer Product Safety Commission Communications Office.

National **Maternal and Child Health** Clearinghouse, 3520 Prospect Street NW., Suite 1, Washington, DC 20057; (202) 625-8410. Provides information and publications on maternal and child health to consumers and health professionals.

National Institute of **Mental Health,** Science Communications Branch, Public Inquiries Section, Parklawn Building, Room 15C-17, 5600 Fishers Lane, Rockville, MD 20857; (301) 443-4513. Distributes Institute publications. Provides referrals to mental health facilities.

Clearinghouse for **Occupational Safety and Health** Information, Technical Information Branch, 4676 Columbia Parkway, Cincinnati, OH 45226; (513) 684-8326. Provides technical support for National Institute for Occupational Safety and Health research programs and supplies information to others on request.

President's Council on **Physical Fitness** and Sports, 450 5th Street NW., Suite 7103, Washington, DC 20001; (202) 272-3430. Conducts a public service advertising program and cooperates with governmental and private groups to promote the development of physical fitness leadership, facilities, and programs. Produces informational materials on exercise, school physical education programs, sports, and physical fitness for youth, adults, and the elderly.

Poison Control Branch, Food and Drug Administration, Parklawn Building, Room 15B-23, 5600 Fishers Lane, Rockville, MD 20857; (301) 443-6260. Works with the national network of 600 poison control centers to reduce the incidence and severity of poisoning. Directs toxic emergency calls to a local poison control center.

Consumer **Product Safety** Commission, Washington, DC 20207; (800) 638-CPSC. Evaluates the safety of products sold to the public. Provides printed materials on different aspects of consumer product safety on request. Does not answer questions from consumers on drugs, prescriptions, warranties, advertising, repairs, or maintenance.

Office on **Smoking** and Health, Technical Information Center, Park Building, Room 1-16, 5600 Fishers Lane, Rockville, MD 20857; (301) 443-1690. Offers bibliographic and reference services to researchers and others, and publishes and distributes a number of titles about smoking.

Sudden Infant Death Syndrome Clearinghouse, 3520 Prospect Street NW., Suite 1, Washington, DC 20057; (202) 625-8400. Provides information on SIDS to health professionals and consumers.

Selected National Organizations

Association for the Advancement of Health Education
1900 Association Drive, Reston, VA 22091
(703) 476-3481

Selected publications
- *Health Education* (journal published bimonthly)
- *The Drug Alternative*
- *Health Education Teaching Ideas: Elementary*
- *Health Education Teaching Ideas: Secondary*
- *Managing Teacher Stress and Burnout*
- *Microcomputers and Health Education*
- *Who Teaches Health?*

American School Health Association
Kent, OH 44240
(216) 678-1601

Selected publications
- *Journal of School Health* (published ten times per year)
- *A Healthy Child: The Key to the Basics*
- *Health Instruction: Guidelines for Planning Health Education Programs, K–12*
- *Mental Health in the Classroom*

National Center for Health Education
30 East 29th Street
New York, NY 10016
(212) 689-1886

Selected publications
- *CENTER* (journal published five times per year)
- *Education for Health: The Selective Guide* (Note: Each CESA human growth and development coordinator has a copy of this guide.)
- *Growing Healthy: Comprehensive Education-for-Health, Grades K–7.*

American Medical Association
Department of Health Education
535 North Dearborn Street
Chicago, IL 60610
(312) 751-6000

Selected publications
- *Physician's Guide to the School Health Curriculum Process*
- *Why Health Education in Your School*

Resources/State

Wisconsin Department of Public Instruction (DPI)
125 South Webster Street
P.O. Box 7841
Madison, WI 53707

Personnel

- Health Education Supervisor
  (608) 266-7032
- School Nursing and Health Services Supervisor
  (608) 266-8857
- Alcohol and Other Drug Abuse Supervisor
  Prevention: (608) 267-9354
  Intervention: (608) 267-9242
  Alcohol and Traffic Safety: (608) 267-9239
- Nutrition Education and Training Coordinator
  (608) 267-9120
- School Social Work Services and School-Age Mothers Program Supervisor
  (608) 266-7921

Selected DPI publications

- *A Continuous Path Toward a School Health Education Program*
  (608) 266-7032
- *Nutrition for Health–An Instructional Package for Grades K–6*
  (608) 267-9120
- *Nutrition in Teenage Pregnancy–A Curriculum Guide*
  (608) 267-9120
- *Child Sexual Assault and Abuse: Guidelines for Schools*
  (608) 266-7921

Wisconsin Department of Health and Social Services
Division of Health, Bureau of Community Health
  and Prevention
P.O. Box 309
Madison, WI 53701
(608) 266-1251

Wisconsin Educational Communications Board
3319 West Beltline Highway, Manager of School Services
Madison, WI 53713-2899
(608) 273-5500

(See listing of ITV health education programs.)

Wisconsin Coalition for School Health Education

This coalition represents more than 20 state-level professional and volunteer organizations with the common purpose of coordinating support for the establishment of comprehensive K–12 health instruction programs in all Wisconsin schools. In 1984 the coalition published a *Resource Directory* which identifies agencies and organizations in Wisconsin that have supplementary print and audiovisual resources to support instruction in the ten major content areas recommended in this guide. A copy of the *Resource Directory* is available free from the

Dairy Council of Wisconsin
13000 West Bluemound Road
Elm Grove, WI 53122
(414) 785-2597

The following organizations or agencies have identified resources in this directory.

American Cancer Society–Milwaukee Division, Inc.
American Cancer Society–Wisconsin Division
American Diabetes Association
American Heart Association
American Lung Association of Wisconsin
American Red Cross–Greater Milwaukee Chapter
Arthritis Foundation–Wisconsin Chapter
City of Milwaukee Health Department–Division of Health Education
Dairy Council of Wisconsin, Inc.
Great Lakes Hemophilia Foundation
Health Education Department–University of Wisconsin–LaCrosse
Juvenile Diabetes Foundation
Leukemia Society of America, Inc.–Wisconsin Chapter
March of Dimes Birth Defects Foundation
Mental Health Association of Wisconsin
National Society to Prevent Blindness–Wisconsin Chapter
Planned Parenthood of Wisconsin
State Medical Society of Wisconsin
United Cerebral Palsy of Wisconsin, Inc.
Wisconsin Association for Health, Physical Education, Recreation, and Dance
Wisconsin Chapter, Cystic Fibrosis Foundation
Wisconsin Clearinghouse
Wisconsin Dental Association
Wisconsin Dental Hygienists' Association
Wisconsin Division of Health
Wisconsin Hospital Association
Wisconsin Human Genetics Education Center
Wisconsin League for Nursing

Resources/Regional and Local

Cooperative Educational Service Agencies (CESAs)

Wisconsin has 12 CESAs throughout the state. Each agency has a Human Growth and Development (HGD) Program primarily responsible for assisting local school districts in the development and implementation of HGD curricula and for providing inservice opportunities for teachers and other school staff. In addition, each CESA makes available to the schools both print and audiovisual resources to support instruction in human growth and development and in most other health education content areas as well.

School staff can obtain assistance by writing or calling the CESA human growth and development coordinator in their area.

CESA #1
P.O. Box 27529
West Allis, WI 53227
(414) 546–3000

CESA #2
4243 Rotamer Road
Janesville, WI 53545
(608) 868–4717

CESA #3
Route 1, Industrial Drive
P.O. Box 5A
Fennimore, WI 53809
(608) 822–3276

CESA #4
LaCrosse County Courthouse
LaCrosse, WI 54601
(608) 785–9364

CESA #5
626 East Slifer Street
P.O. Box 564
Portage, WI 53901
(608) 742–8811

CESA #6
P.O. Box 2568
Oshkosh, WI 54903
(414) 233–2372

CESA #7
2280A South Broadway
Green Bay, WI 54304
(414) 457–3755

CESA #8
Lake and Main
Gillet, WI 54124
(414) 855–2114

CESA #9
P.O. Box 449
328 North 4th Street
Tomahawk, WI 54487
(715) 453–2141

CESA #10
725 West Park Avenue
Chippewa Falls, WI 54729
(715) 723–0341

CESA #11
P.O. Box 728
Cumberland, WI 54829
(715) 822–4711

CESA #12
502 West 2nd Street
Ashland, WI 54806
(715) 682–2316

Selected Local Resources

Most counties and cities have health-related agencies and organizations which can provide consultation, speakers, and materials to schools. The following is a selected sample of some of these resources.

City, county, and state health departments
Sanitarians
Health educators
Public health nurses
Environmental engineers
Dietitians and nutritionists
Health commissioners

Hospitals, clinics, and health centers
Nursing personnel
Physicians
Physical therapists
Inhalation therapists
Laboratory technologists
Paramedics and physician assistants
Medical records librarians
Dentists
Dental hygienists and assistants
Patient educators

Emergency medical personnel
Rescue squad workers
Firefighters
Ambulance personnel
Red Cross first-aid instructors
Emergency medical technicians

Mental health workers
Psychologists
Psychiatric social workers
Family counselors
Psychiatrists
Crisis center workers
School guidance counselors

Other health personnel
School nurses
Pharmacists
School health educators
Ophthalmologists
Optometrists

Agencies and organizations
Red Cross
Mental health center
Heart Association
Cancer Society
Arthritis Foundation
Office on Aging
Alcoholics Anonymous
Lung Association
Soil Conservation Service
Environmental Protection Agency
Comprehensive health planning agency
Hospital auxiliary

Resources/Instructional Television
(ITV) Programs

Sources of Information

The ITV health education series listed in this section are broadcast statewide each year over the Wisconsin Educational Television Network. In addition to broadcasting its programs, the network grants taping rights to allow teachers the flexibility to use regular instructional series at times convenient to them.

At the beginning of each school year, a new broadcast schedule of dates and times for each series is available from the health education supervisor, Wisconsin Department of Public Instruction, 125 South Webster Street, P.O. Box 7841, Madison, WI 53707; (608) 266-7032

Additional information concerning ITV series and teacher guides is available from the following ITV regional service units.

Channel 9 (ITFS)/Milwaukee Public Schools
Director of Instructional Resources
P.O. Drawer 10K
Milwaukee, WI 53201
(414) 475-8143

Channel 36/Milwaukee area
Southeastern Wisconsin In-School Telecommunications (SEWIST)
c/o CESA 1
P.O. Box 27529
West Allis, WI 53227
(414) 546-3000

Channel 38 area and Channel 20 area east of Highway 51 *(also serves Translator 55/Ellison Bay area)*
Northeastern Wisconsin In-School Telecommunications (NEWIST)
Instructional Services Bldg.
UW–Green Bay
Green Bay, WI 54302
(414) 465-2599

Channel 21 area
Southern Wisconsin Educational Communications Service (SWECS)
c/o CESA 2
3319 W. Beltline Highway
Madison, WI 53713
(608) 221-6223

Channel 31 area *(also serves Translator 49/Bloomington area)*
Western Wisconsin Broadcast Instruction Council (WWBIC)
c/o CESA 4
205 Main Street
Onalaska, WI 54650
(608) 785-9373

Channel 36/Park Falls area and Channel 8 area
Lake Superior Broadcast Instruction Council (LSBIC)
Channel 8
1202 East University Circle
Duluth, MN 55811
(218) 724-8568

Channel 28 area and Channel 20 area west of Highway 51 *(also serves Translator 55/River Falls area)*
Northwest Instruction Broadcast Service (NIBS)
c/o CESA 11
P.O. Box 158
Elmwood, WI 54740
(715) 232-1627

ITV Programs

Grades K-1
Strawberry Square
Music/Health Ed ● Thirty-three 15-minute programs

This series provides opportunities for young children to experience music. A wide variety of creative playful experiences are associated with the basic elements of music. The series aims to promote creativity, musical enjoyment, and an aesthetic orientation to the physical world along with healthy social relations and an understanding of the rules and routines of school.

Grades K-2
All About You
Health Education ● Thirty 15-minute programs

All About You explains human anatomy, physiology, and psychology on a level that youngsters can understand. The series shows how people grow and develop and why people should care about their health.

The format resembles the original award-winning series, **All About You,** but incorporates a greater variety of visual materials and on-location recording.

Grades K-3
Like You, Like Me
Health Education ● Ten 10-minute programs

Using a cast of animated characters, each of the programs dramatizes one or more handicapping conditions and sets the tone for acceptance and understanding of the handicapped child by encouraging recognition of the inner qualities that make each person special.

Grades 1-3
Calling All Safety Scouts
Health Education ● Six 15-minute programs

Every child experiences some kind of accident, whether it be touching a hot iron, incurring minor cuts and bruises in a playground fall, or being involved in a more serious accident on a farm, in the street, or in the water. Accidents do not just "happen"; they are generally the results of carelessness or lack of knowledge about safety practices.

Calling All Safety Scouts is designed to make children aware of safety practices at home, at school, and in the neighborhood. Programs stress the need to stop accidents before they happen and encourage children to develop a positive, responsible attitude which can help them face the risks of everyday life, yet still allow them to have fun.

The fast-moving magazine format uses puppets, songs, riddles, quizzes, and limericks to reinforce safety information.

Grades 1-3
Well, Well, Well
with Slim Goodbody
Health Education ● Fifteen 15-minute programs

Children like to be in charge, especially of things that concern them. Even young children in the primary grades can take an active part in protecting, maintaining, and improving their own good health. In this series, Slim Goodbody, late of the ITV network's **The Inside Story with Slim Goodbody** and **Captain Kangaroo,** shows them how to take responsibility for feeling good.

Food, first aid, and feelings are stressed more than blood and bones in this approach to health education. The lively programs balance entertainment with solid content about healthful living.

Grades 3-4
The Inside Story
with Slim Goodbody
Health Education • Eight 15-minute programs

People all carry an amazing story within them—the story of how human bodily systems work. In this series, Slim Goodbody tells children the inside story about their own bodies.

Students may be familiar with body-suited Slim from his appearances on the preschool TV series **Captain Kangaroo.** In this in-school series, Slim uses animated narration, memorable songs, and huge working models of body systems to make third through fifth graders aware of how their systems function and how they can take care of their bodies.

The series has received awards from the National Association of Educational Broadcasters, the Milan Film Festival, the Athens Video Festival, the Birmingham Educational Film Festival, the Chicago International Film Festival, and the International Film and TV Festival of New York. **The Inside Story with Slim Goodbody** was produced for the Wisconsin Educational Television Network by the UW–Green Bay Center for Television Production.

Grades 3-5
Inside/Out
Health Education • Thirty 15-minute programs

Designed by health educators and learning specialists, this interdisciplinary series helps eight- to ten-year-olds understand and cope with their emotions. Using dramatizations and documentaries to portray experiences common to young lives, the programs deal with social, emotional, and physical problems. **Inside/Out** aims to help young people develop coping skills that can serve throughout adult life. The affective approach helps children understand their own sadness, happiness, joy, fear, love, and hate, as well as those same feelings in others.

Inside/Out is the winner of an Emmy Award for instructional children's programming.

Grades 4-6
Who Cares...
Health Education • Eight 20-minute programs

Who cares... takes an holistic approach to health care. Students see that they are responsible for their own "wellness," and that decision making, coping skills, and lifestyle affect their physical and emotional well-being.

Produced by Northeastern Wisconsin In-School Television (NEWIST), this series lets children in the Green Bay area speak spontaneously. Viewers will hear some refreshingly candid observations by fifth and sixth graders.

Grades 5-6
High Feather
Health Education • Ten 30-minute programs

In this series, a group of four girls and four boys at a summer camp realize that good nutritional habits can help them perform in a race, a dance competition, and other situations. Seeing the link between eating well and feeling fit should motivate viewers to eat food that's good for them. The series stresses that each person must take the responsibility for how he or she eats.

Grades 6-8
Terra: Our World
Environmental Education • Ten 20-minute programs

Grades 7-8
Jackson Junior High
Health Education • Four 15-minute programs

Grades 7-9
Self, Incorporated
Health Education • Fifteen 15-minute programs

Grades 9-12
On the Level
Health Education • Twelve 15-minute programs

Grades 9-12
Your Diet
Health Education • Six 15-minute programs

Terra: Our World attempts to make students aware of environmental problems and get them involved in solving such problems. Television newswoman Connie Chung introduces a major environmental topic at the start of each program. Interviews, explanations, and on-site visits follow. The series examines the scientific, aesthetic, social, and economic implications of each issue.

Jackson Junior High aims to make youngsters responsible about alcohol so that they can function comfortably as drinkers or abstainers and so that they may be able to assist relatives or friends who abuse alcohol.

Students in grades 7 and 8 may have experimented with an alcoholic drink or two, but most have not yet had to choose whether or not to drink. By the time these youngsters reach high school, however, most of them will have experienced peer pressure to drink and may be stimulated by their own curiosity about alcohol. Alcohol education can help students prepare for decisions about whether and how much to drink.

Self, Incorporated helps early adolescents cope with the emotional and social problems that arise from their physical and social changes. Privacy, dating readiness, peer group pressures, male and female role identities, cliques, and families are just a few of the topics examined.

Self, Incorporated helps teachers and other adults to stimulate students to reflect on and talk candidly about their concerns, to become aware of the choices available to them, and to understand the consequences of their actions.

The years from 14 through 17 are a time of emotional and physical change, of personal and social growth. The **On the Level** health series encourages students to be more aware of and active in shaping their personal and social growth.

Programs help teenagers learn how to take better care of themselves and others, to manage their emotional health, and to deal constructively with change and other sources of stress.

Your Diet makes students aware of how what they do or neglect to do can affect their bodies and what they can do to live healthier—and happier—lives.

"Think before you take another bite of that double-fudge, creme-filled torte or sit listening to music rather than dancing to it!" the series suggests.

The evidence is mounting that lifestyle—exercise, food, and health habits—can affect everyone's health now and in the future.

185

Practical Principles in the
Effective Use of Print Materials

This article is excerpted from the volume Mental Health Education: Principles in the
Effective Use of Materials *by Nina Ridenour, Ph.D., published a number of years ago by
the Mental Health Materials Center. It is reprinted with permission of the copyright owner
from* Education-for-Health: The Selective Guide, *published by the National Center for
Health Education. It comprises a series of lecture-discussions presented over a period of
several years before many groups of health educators and mental health professionals
throughout the United States. The principles and criteria remain of practical value and
guidance to those carrying out education-for-health activities. These excerpts are taken
largely from the first two chapters of this work. Dr. Ridenour served as the Mental Health
Materials Center's chief consultant from 1953 until she retired in 1969.*

The purpose of this discussion is not to specify what materials to use, and still less to
spell out how to run a program, but to set forth certain principles in the selection and use
of materials likely to increase their effectiveness.

One might think that the importance of using good materials would be self-evident.
But it is not. If it were, surely so much poor stuff would not be floating around.

Selection of sound and appropriate materials requires thoughtful planning. The
effectiveness of education for health is enhanced in direct relation to the sensitive,
knowledgeable, and creative use of materials.

Assessing the Content

In practice the effective use of materials can be guided by a simple concept, "Good of
its kind," supported by five basic criteria.

The Concept

"Good of its kind" is the concept of trying to judge the item, whatever it is, *in terms of
the purpose it is intended to serve.* This allows wide flexibility and yet implies some
standard of excellence, comparable to judging a work of art for itself. It serves as a
framework for your own value judgments. You may suddenly see—become sensitive
to—a new potential in an item, perhaps a new program angle you had not thought of
before. Or if you conclude that the item is not "good of its kind," you may feel spurred to
look further and try to find something that is up to your standards, instead of being
willing to accept something inferior because it is the only thing you happen to know about
at the moment. In applying the "good of its kind" concept it is helpful to consider basic
criteria which combine objective measures and subjective opinion. Here are five basic
qualities to look for when assessing educational materials:

- Substance
- Validity
- Balance
- Authority
- Integrity

If any item has these five qualities, it is *probably* a pretty good piece of material. If it lacks any one of these to any marked degree, then it may be wise to take another look, although you may have special reasons for using it despite its deficiencies.

Substance

To satisfy the criterion of *substance*, the item *must say something*. More than that, the item must *show evidence of being derived from an organized body of knowledge*. Mental health and, increasingly, health, are fields in which many people are writing who have no competence in the subjects whatever. Ask yourself: Is this something just anybody could have written off the top of his or her head? Or does it reflect a sound background of knowledge?

Furthermore, the material can be ever so *popular* in style, but *it must not be superficial*. Sound, even profound, ideas can be dressed up in professional jargon. Popular means *for the people*. Superficial means lacking in depth.

Validity

The second criterion is *validity*—and the derivation of the word is relevant here. It comes from words meaning *to be strong, to be of worth* and according to the dictionary means something founded on truth or fact, capable of being supported or justified or defended. As used here, it means that the information is *capable of being supported or justified* in the opinion of trained and experienced persons. Another way of saying this is that the item *must be sound as our present state of knowledge* permits. This implies, further, that it must not contain any outright inaccuracies or distortions.

Common distorting qualities can be divided into several categories:
- misrepresentations, including out-and-out errors of fact.
- oversimplification both in advice-giving and in the interpretation of ideas.
- attributing an effect to the wrong cause or jumping at conclusions on insufficient evidence.

Balance

Balance is best described in terms of its opposite, imbalance. This means any excess, any extreme, any exaggeration, incomplete thought, half-truth, or significant omission, any statement that should be qualified and is not.

When dealing with complex ideas, there are many times when flat statements are not permissible, when you positively must qualify: *"Some people do so and so," "Sometimes* this or that . . . ," "In *some* circumstances . . . ," "It *may* be . . ." The dramatic writers hate these words. They call them "weasel words" and it is true they do tend to make writing ponderous. But better a little dullness than sweeping or inaccurate generalizations that cannot be supported and for that matter might very well cause harm.

Authority

The *authority* behind a piece of material is a sort of negative safeguard. Good authority does not assure a good piece of material, and at times it happens that very bad materials are turned out under very good auspices and by able authorities. But good authority increases the likelihood that a piece of material is good. If the item shows no

187

evidence of any kind of authority behind it, then be suspicious. That does not mean it is bad. Nor does it mean don't use it. But do inspect it carefully.

Some of the details it is a good idea to look for when questioning authority are: Who is the author? What is his or her training or specialization? Are any degrees indicated - M.D., Ph.D., M.P.H., R.N.? Is there an organization behind the item? Is it an organization qualified in the field under discussion? What is the evidence of authority?

Integrity

Integrity is the most controversial and the hardest of the criteria to talk about. Integrity as used here means that the motivation behind a piece is what it purports to be; that there is no motive antithetical to sound principles of mental health or education.

The most frequent of the ulterior motives is publicity, by itself a completely legitimate motive, an entirely proper reason for producing certain types of material. We have to have things written specifically for publicity, for promotion, for fund-raising; things that interpret facts, ideas, concepts to the public; things that interpret the work of agencies, institutions, and organizations. But an awful lot of confusion has arisen between education on the one side and public relations on the other. Most of the confusion comes about because the two fields are like two intersecting circles that have a certain area in common while each circle has an area it does not share with the other.

Among the abuses, one of the most regrettable is *appealing to people's needs and emotions when not justified.* People long for happiness, for freedom from anxiety, for financial security, for professional success, for social success, for marital harmony, for peace of mind—the list goes on indefinitely. Much of the popular health literature *promises* such things to them if only they will *read this pamphlet* or *memorize that list* or *this set of rules* or *see that film*, or *talk it out with somebody.*

Such promises are not justified. The same is true for tearjerkers. Warm human stories about the tragedies of illness can be used to advantage in interpretation. But drippy sentimentality rarely has a place in effective education.

Educational materials must maintain integrity. No extraneous motive such as the desire for publicity or wide distribution must be allowed to usurp the educational standards of honesty, accuracy, soundness. When goals conflict, and the true motivation for a piece is other than it purports, look out for subtle and insidious implications.

Assessing the Presentation

The way something is presented—"how you say it"—should be shaped at least in part by the "to whom." Who is the audience you are speaking to? Again and again the literature of the field sounds as if the writer had completely forgotten the audience for whom the material is intended. This might be called "The Case of the Forgotten Audience."

If the writer is not thinking about his readers, what then is he thinking about? Sometimes you can tell that he is concentrating exclusively on what *he* wishes to say, regardless of who is likely to read it. In other words he is writing—not to teach—but to express himself. This may be a good way to produce a work of art—poetry, essays, creative writing—but can it be depended upon to produce good educational material? I would say: only occasionally.

Sometimes the writer is not overly concerned with self-expression but totally absorbed in his subject—call it *subject orientation*. The result is that he will probably include a lot of extraneous material not appropriate for his readership, much of which could be omitted to advantage.

And then sometimes you can tell that the writer is thinking only of his peers. He talks in language *only* they could be expected to understand, with the result that the *only* people who can understand it are those who could have written it in the first place. Of course each of these three orientations has its place: self-expression in creative writing; subject orientation in an encyclopedia article or textbook; peer orientation in a professional journal. But any one of these when carried to extremes is likely to interfere with the effectiveness of the material as an educational tool.

There are three additional criteria to keep in mind in order to keep the materials oriented to the audience:

- definition of audience
- appropriateness
- internal consistency

Definition of Audience

Who is the audience? To *whom* are you speaking? Is the audience defined—not necessarily in words—but by implication?

The effectiveness of education, for example, is enhanced when it is directed to *homogeneous, highly motivated groups*. Sometimes there is misunderstanding about what constitutes such a group. For instance, a neighborhood group, or a church group, or a PTA group, in which the children cover a wide age range, though homogeneous in certain respects such as education or cultural background or community concerns, may not be homogeneous with respect to health or health problems or interests. Examples of homogeneous, highly motivated groups are parents of first-born infants, engaged couples, families of patients with a particular health problem, and the like.

In general, anything that is outstandingly good for a restricted audience invariably finds a variety of uses and ends up by reaching a larger audience than anticipated.

Appropriateness

Examples of inappropriateness occur when the writer tosses in irrelevancies, derogates an entire category of people, such as teachers, or physicians, or psychologists, or parents. Still other types of inappropriateness are cynicism tossed in gratuitously and, obviously, bad jokes about the audience.

That brings us to the question of satire. Does satire have a place in health education? With an occasional rare exception it does not. The genius of satire lies in the way it often illumines human foibles with profound insight. It *can* be free of rancor and hostility. But it rarely is! And that is my main point. Ordinarily, one does not have to analyze satire very carefully to recognize the undercurrent of cynicism and hostility. It masquerades as humor. People may laugh, but notice how often the laugh is self-conscious, apologetic, embarrassed. They are not laughing because they feel gay or relieved or entertained. They are laughing because a point has struck home and they wish to cover up their true feelings. As a device, satire more often than not, tends to make people feel uncomfortable, ill at ease, self-conscious, less adequate, less whole, less accepting. Is *that* the goal of health education?

Internal Consistency

Materials should not be addressed to mutually exclusive levels of understanding. If in the same publication you include both very simple and very complex or technical information, you may find that the part of your material that is simple enough for one audience is too simple for the other and vice versa. Thus you fall between two stools. You are either talking down to part of your audience or talking over the heads of the other part.

Assessing the Quality of Writing

Frequently communication failure can be traced to poor writing. With respect to the quality of writing the criteria that can be applied are:

Clarity

Among the faults interfering with clarity are jargon, bad syntax, bad structure, ponderousness, unnecessary technicalities, and the like.

Jargon, in particular, is an offender against clarity. Jargon, meaning the technical or secret vocabulary of a science, along with a couple of its less polite synonyms, lingo and gibberish, is among the worst faults of professional writing. It has a way of quickly finding its way into popular writing as well.

Tone

It is curious how often a vaguely disagreeable note creeps into health and mental health writing. The substance and the content may be good but the tone is just plain unpleasant. Such a tone creeps into a lot of writing for parents, especially in the form of *blaming*, or when the writer is obviously *taking sides*—parents versus children.

Other points to be mentioned about tone are talking down to the audience and humor at the expense of the audience. If humor is not light, then skip it. And the same thing goes for trying to be *cute*, or any other striving for effect. If you have to reach for it, don't.

Organization

Material can, of course, be over-organized: "My first point . . . My second point . . . My third point . . ." When overdone this leads to heavy reading. But on the whole far more errors are committed by insufficient or careless organization than by over-organization.

Does the material get into the subject quickly? How many readers do you suppose are lost by long meandering introductions? Then if on top of an introduction you add a preface and a foreword and a string of acknowledgments—good-bye reader.

Assessing the Medium and Format

The written word and the spoken word are two different media—a point that seems to be forgotten all too often, especially in this day of electronic communication. When one is transposed verbatim to the other, something is lost and there are few exceptions. Much regrettable waste of money and energy is to be found in verbatim reports of meetings and discussions. You have a meeting, you set up a tape recorder or hire a stenotypist if your budget permits, you get a transcription, somebody does a bit of touch-up editing, and off it goes to the printer. That is the easy way, and rarely worth the paper it is written on. *You cannot embalm the flavor of a discussion that way*, and you might as well not try.

With respect to format, a detail to be careful about is odd sizes and shapes. If something comes in that is so large or so queer a shape that it will not go into a standard file drawer and will not fit on a standard bookshelf, then it belongs in the round file—the wastebasket. Sometimes the excessively small things are a nuisance too. Also be careful about things that are too gimmicky, or try too hard to be *arty* (in contradistinction to artistic).

Leaflets with complex folds can be a nuisance, as confusing as refolding a road map. Also, since in our culture we read from left to right, it seems a good idea to stick to that, even in publicity pieces. Another good idea is to have the front cover on the front and not on the back.

The *right* print material can be an important program aid. When content is accurate and presentation a balanced one in harmony with the characteristics of the intended audience, printed material can serve a variety of purposes. For example it can introduce new ideas, correct information, and reinforce information provided verbally. Therefore, time invested in the review and selection process utilizing a range of criteria is time well spent because the decisions made and judgments reached influence both program outcome and budgetary outlay.

Although all of the material that appears in this volume has been reviewed and selected based on the concept *good of its kind* and the criteria discussed here, one task remains. That is for the definitive user to *fine tune* the selection to match as precisely as possible available materials with specific program objectives and target group needs.

Checklist for Evaluating a School Health Education Program*

KEY: A = COMPLETELY
B = SOMEWHAT
C = NOT AT ALL

Criteria	A	B	C	Recommended Action
A. POLICY AND CURRICULUM The district has a planned health education program with identified goals, objectives, and scope and sequence of instruction for grade levels consistent with the current state curriculum guidelines.				
1. A written statement of the district's policy regarding the health education program is available.				
2. The district has a health education curriculum consistent with the current state health instruction guidelines.				
a. The health education curriculum is up to date.				
b. The health education curriculum includes a statement about health education philosophy, grade-level objectives, and scope and sequence of content.				
3. Responsibilities are defined for all persons involved in the health education program (principals, teachers, school nurses, and others).				
B. STAFF The district has assigned personnel to provide leadership for the implementation and maintenance of a comprehensive health education program and has provided the necessary resources.				
1. A person at the district level has been named health education coordinator with delegated responsibility for providing leadership to the district health education coordinating team.				
a. The district coordinator and coordinating team are provided with time and support to carry out duties.				
2. The person with primary leadership responsibility has interest and professional preparation in health education.				

This checklist is adapted from: *Criteria for Evaluating the School Health Education Program*
California State Department of Education
School Health Program Component
Sacramento, California 1977

Criteria	A	B	C	Recommended Action
3. The person with leadership responsibility coordinates school health education activities with community health activities, working with representatives of official and volunteer health agencies, professional health associations, and other groups concerned with health education.				
4. The district provides the resources (funding, personnel, materials) necessary to operate the health education program.				
C. COMMUNITY INPUT AND RESOURCES Health education programs are coordinated with community health programs. Representatives of public and private agencies and organizations, as well as students and parents, are involved in the planning and/or implementation of the program.				
1. An active school and community health education advisory group is involved in planning, implementing, and/or evaluating the school health education program.				
2. Students are involved in planning, implementing, and/or evaluating the school health education program.				
3. Parents are involved in planning, implementing, and/or evaluating the school health education program.				
4. A guide or directory is available and includes information about community and district resources which support health education.				
5. Community and district resources are screened and evaluated for possible use for inservice training programs in health education.				
6. Teachers are aware of health counseling and health service resources provided by the district and the community.				
7. The community is utilized as a laboratory for student experiences in health education.				

Criteria	A	B	C	Recommended Action
D. STAFF QUALIFICATIONS AND INSERVICE Persons who provide instruction in health education have had professional preparation in health education through preservice or inservice training.				
1. Opportunities for inservice training in health education are available to staff members, support staff, and others.				
2. Teachers are involved in the planning of the inservice training programs.				
3. Inservice training opportunities in health education receive emphasis comparable to that given to inservice training opportunities in other academic subject areas.				
4. Teachers at the elementary and secondary levels other than health instructors have had preservice or inservice preparation in health education.				
5. Those teaching health courses in junior and senior high schools have a major, minor, and/or master's in health education.				
6. The district supports and provides health promotion activities for the staff.				
E. INSTRUCTION–ORGANIZATION The educational experience of each student in the elementary school and in the secondary school includes identifiable health instruction.				
1. The philosophy, goals, and objectives for health instruction are consistent with those included in the current state health instruction guidelines.				
2. Objectives in terms of student knowledge, attitudes, and behavior related to health have been established at each grade level.				
3. Specific time is allocated for health instruction to achieve stated objectives.				

Criteria	A	B	C	Recommended Action
4. Health instruction is integrated and corre-lated with other subject areas when such practice will achieve stated health education objectives.				
5. Credit equal to that given for instruction in other academic subjects is given for health instruction.				
6. At the elementary level, the health instruction program is coordinated within the total instructional program.				
7. Students at the junior high school level (except students excused) receive discrete health instruction for at least one semester or the equivalent.				
8. Students at the senior high school (9-12) level (except students excused) receive discrete health instruction as a graduation require-ment for at least one semester meeting daily or the equivalent.				
9. Students at the senior high school level have the opportunity to select an elective course in health education.				
F. INSTRUCTION–ACTIVITIES/METHODS Health instruction focuses upon attitudes and problem solving as well as knowledge.				
1. A balance exists between attitude develop-ment and cognitive approaches to health education in the classroom.				
2. Instructional activities are planned and devel-oped in such a way as to enable students to: a. grow in self-awareness; that is, develop a positive sense of identity and self-esteem;				
b. develop skills for effective decision making;				
c. grow in coping skills; that is, apply learning in daily living.				

Criteria	A	B	C	Recommended Action
3. The following methods are used separately or in combination when appropriate. 　a. Problem solving				
b. Demonstration				
c. Laboratory experimentation				
d. Lecture-discussion				
e. Reading and writing projects				
f. Discussion – large and small group				
g. Student projects				
h. Research				
i. Community projects				
G. INSTRUCTION–CONTENT The content of health education is designed to serve current and future student health needs.				
1. Content centers on health promotion/wellness, prevention, and maintenance of positive health rather than illness, disease, and problems.				
2. The major content includes the following, and the degree of emphasis on each area is based on assessed needs of students. 　a. Accident prevention and safety				
b. Community health				
c. Consumer health				
d. Environmental health				
e. Family life education				
f. Mental and emotional health				
g. Nutrition				
h. Personal health				
i. Prevention and control of disease				
j. Substance use and abuse				

Criteria	A	B	C	Recommended Action
H. MATERIALS–RESOURCES Materials used in health education are current and accurate.				
1. Materials are up to date.				
2. Materials are scientifically accurate.				
3. Materials are selected for their contribution to meeting objectives of the health education program.				
4. Instruction is enriched by the use of materials available from official and volunteer health agencies and professional associations.				
5. Instruction is enriched by the use of current audiovisual materials, such as films, film-strips, models, charts, radio and TV programs, and tape recordings.				
I. EVALUATION A plan exists for evaluating the health education program.				
1. A planned program of evaluation will appraise the effectiveness of health education in terms of student growth in: a. knowledge related to health,				
b. attitudes toward health and health practices,				
c. present and future health actions.				
2. The results of evaluations are used to continuously improve the health education programs.				

Note: For additional program evaluation guidelines , contact

University of Wisconsin-Madison
School Evaluation Services
Room 427, Education Building
Madison, WI 53706
(608) 263-5656

Wisconsin Statutes/School Health Education

The following state statutes (ss.) and administrative rules affect health education in Wisconsin schools. For further clarification of these laws and rules, contact the Department of Public Instruction health education supervisor.

I. (1985) 121.02 (1) (j) Health Instruction. Ensure that instruction in elementary and high schools in health, physical education, art and music is provided by qualified teachers.

   (j) the administrative rule or the criteria for this particular standard is as follows:
   - Health instruction shall be provided in accordance with a written comprehensive health education curriculum which includes the curricular areas defined in ss. 115.35 (1) and 118.01 (2)* of the Wisconsin Statutes.
   - A professional staff member shall be designated as coordinator of health education.
   - Health education in grades K-6 shall be under the supervision of a Department certified health teacher.
   - In grades 7-12 health education shall be conducted by or under the supervision of a Department certified health teacher and shall include one structured course in health taught by a Department certified health teacher.

   *(Recreated in 1983 in Wisconsin Act 412, as 118.01 Educational Goals and Expectations, (d) Personal development.)

II. (1983) Wisconsin Act 412 repeals curriculum requirements found in ss. 118.01. Section 3 of this new law was recreated to read as follows.

   118.01 **Educational Goals and Expectations.** This section of the law substitutes educational goals and expectations for the old curriculum requirements included within 118.01. The goals and expectations are divided into categories of: (a) academic skills and knowledge; (b) vocational skills; (c) citizenship; and (d) personal development. The most significant impact on school health education is found under the category of personal development. That entire category as printed in the law is as follows.

   (d) Personal development. Each school board shall provide an instructional program designed to give pupils:

   1. The skills needed to cope with social change.
   2. Knowledge of the human body and the means to maintain lifelong health, including:
      a. Knowledge of the theory and practice of physical education, including the development and maintenance of physical fitness;

b. Knowledge of the true and comparative vitamin content of food and health values of dairy products and their importance for the human diet; and

c. Knowledge of physiology and hygiene, sanitation, the effects of controlled substances under ch. 161 and alcohol upon the human system, symptoms of disease and the proper care of the body. No pupil may be required to take instruction in these subjects if his or her parent files with the teacher a written objection thereto. Instruction in physiology and hygiene shall include instruction on sexually transmitted diseases and shall be offered in every high school.

3. An appreciation of artistic and creative expression and the capacity for self-expression.

4. The ability to construct personal ethics and goals.

5. Knowledge of morality and the individual's responsibility as a social being, including the responsibility and morality of family living and the value of frugality and other basic qualities and principles referred to in article I, section 22, of the constitution insofar as such qualities and principles affect family and consumer education.

6. Knowledge of the prevention of accidents and promotion of safety on the public highways, including instruction on the relationship between highway safety and the use of alcohol and controlled substances under ch. 161.

III. (1983) Wisconsin Act 411 created ss. 118.33, relating to establishing high school graduation requirements. Part of Section 2, 118.33 reads as follows.

118.33 High School Graduation Standards. (1) (a) (intro.) Beginning September 1, 1988, a school board may not grant a high school diploma to any pupil unless the pupil has earned:

1. In the high school grades, at least 4 credits of English including writing composition, 3 credits of social studies including state and local government, 2 credits of mathematics, 2 credits of science, 1.5 credits of physical education.
The state superintendent shall encourage school boards to require an additional 8.5 credits selected from any combination of vocational education, foreign languages, fine arts and other courses.

2. In grades 7 to 12, at least 0.5 credit of health education.
The administrative rule or the criteria for the health education course requirements is as follows:

(g) 0.5 credit of health education which shall incorporate instruction in personal, family, community, and environmental health.

The following are selected definitions included in the administrative rule:

● *Course* means study which has the fundamental purpose of developing the knowledge, concepts, and abilities in a subject.

● *Credit* means the credit given for successful completion of a school term of study in one course in the high school grades that meets daily for a normal class period or the equivalent established by the board.

Certification Requirements for Health Teachers in Wisconsin

Elementary level (K-8)

There is no specific certification requirement related to teaching health education as part of a regular classroom activity.

The Department of Public Instruction strongly recommends that all elementary teacher preparation institutions include health education as part of the preservice preparation for all elementary teachers.

An elementary teacher eligible for a license to teach grade eight may be licensed at the ninth-grade level in areas in which an approved minor has been completed (for example, health education).

Secondary level (7-12)

Certification requirements in health education are the same as for all other academic subject areas (science, math, and so on). A teaching major of at least 34 semester credits, or a teaching minor of at least 22 semester credits if certified in another area with a major, is required.

Currently, the following Wisconsin teacher preparation institutions have approved programs in health education.

Major/Minor/M.S.
University of Wisconsin (UW-La Crosse)

Minor

UW-Madison	UW-Superior
UW-Milwaukee	UW-Whitewater
UW-Oshkosh	Alverno College
UW-Platteville	Carroll College
UW-River Falls	Carthage College
UW-Stevens Point	Ripon College

A one-year special license may be issued if requested by an employing district administrator who must provide full explanation and justification of the need.

Renewal of the special license may be granted upon request of the employing district administrator and upon the applicant's satisfactory completion of a minimum of six semester credits in an approved program between date the special license is issued and date of renewal.

Criteria for Comprehensive School Health Education

The following is an excerpt from a 1984 paper entitled "Comprehensive School Health Education as defined by the National Professional School Health Education Organizations." A complete copy of the paper is available from the Department of Public Instruction health education supervisor.

The term "criteria" as used in this document refers to qualitative or quantitative standards of either performance or design by which a program of comprehensive school health education may be judged. Comprehensive school health programs include health instruction, services, and concern for the quality of the school's physical, social, and emotional environment. However, the statements that follow are concerned solely with aspects of curriculum, administration, and teaching methodology.

A comprehensive school health instructional program is defined by the following.

● *Instruction intended to motivate health maintenance and promote wellness and not merely the prevention of disease or disability*

Comprehensive school health education focuses on the entire continuum of health status and not merely disease identification and prevention. Such education has goals and objectives aimed at assisting students in making the kinds of decisions that can help them build or maintain the best health status possible as well as to eliminate or prevent disease.

● *Activities designed to develop decision-making competencies related to health and health behavior*

Comprehensive school health instruction provides the cognitive information, behavioral skills, and affective experiences necessary for students to more effectively decide which health behavior(s) they will choose. The focus is on the processes the student encounters or participates in as well as the final behavioral outcomes. It does not merely prescribe a set of health behaviors that a student should adopt.

● *A planned, sequential pre-K to 12 curriculum based upon students' needs and current and emerging health concepts and societal issues*

A comprehensive school health education program is designed to meet the specific health needs and interests of all students as they progress through the various (pre-K to 12) grade levels. The learning experiences are based and built upon past learning experiences as a means of ensuring continuity. Health needs and interests vary within any grade level. A comprehensive program is flexible and responsive to changes in the learners and in the social settings in which they live.

● *Opportunities for all students to develop and demonstrate health-related knowledge, attitudes, and practices*

Comprehensive school health education functions in all three domains of learning (cognitive, affective, and psychomotor). The providing of knowledge alone is usually insufficient in addressing all of the complexities of human health status. Thus, comprehensive school health education programs include activities related to the development of feelings, attitudes, and behaviors conducive to good health. It is important that a comprehensive program include a balanced approach in which all three domains are emphasized.

● *Integration of the physical, mental, emotional, and social dimensions of health as the basis for study of the following topic areas*

"Mental health" has always been considered an essential area of health education content. However, comprehensive school health education places greater emphasis on mental health by considering it as an inseparable dimension of health status. As such, comprehensive programs devote substantial curricular time to the mental aspect of *each* topic area.

It is generally accepted that human health consists of at least four dimensions (physical, mental, emotional, and social). A comprehensive school health education program addresses *each* topic area with attention given to each of the four dimensions.

The content of a comprehensive program also is balanced so as to provide adequate coverage to each area somewhere within the entire K-12 curriculum. Emphasis on only a few topic areas is avoided because such an approach fails to address the complex nature of human health and thus is not comprehensive.

The following topic areas are listed in alphabetical order. One does not have precedence over the others.

— Community health
— Consumer health
— Environmental health
— Family life
— Growth and development
— Nutritional health
— Personal health
— Prevention and control of disease and disorders
— Safety and accident prevention
— Substance use and abuse

- *Specific program goals and objectives*

Comprehensive school health education program goals and objectives are clearly stated. They define the nature and character of the curriculum and instruction, and they provide the foundation upon which educational planning and evaluation are based. Objectives are addressed to the needs and interests of students, and reflect that which reasonably can be attained as a result of planned program activities. Objectives are written in measurable terms so that their attainment can be evaluated.

- *Formative and summative evaluation procedures*

Evaluation is essential in providing information on program effectiveness. It furnishes useful information about the quality of instruction, and the comparative needs, status, and progress of students. Evaluation should be continuous and concurrent with program activities as it provides both an inventory of present status and an assessment of progress.

- *An effective management system*

Comprehensive school health education programs are complex. Effective administration of the diverse affairs associated with such programs requires management policies and personnel responsible for the planning, implementation, coordination, and continuation of program activities that are at least equal to those received by other academic disciplines. Without such management, the effectiveness or existence of programs may be compromised.

- *Sufficient resources: budgeted instructional materials, time, management staff, and teachers*

The extent to which comprehensive school health education objectives can be attained is directly dependent upon the nature of the resources provided for such purposes by the school system. Resources include up-to-date instructional materials available for teaching health; the provision of class time equal to that afforded other basic disciplines;

assignment of teachers who are qualified health education specialists by virtue of their professional preparation or as an outcome of extensive inservice or postgraduate study in school health education; and a management system capable of providing the necessary leadership, support, and coordination required to ensure a successful education program.

Nobody sees what I can see

For in back of my eyes there is only me

And nobody knows how my thoughts begin

Because there's only myself inside my skin

Isn't it strange how everyone owns just enough
  skin to cover their bones

My father's would be much too big to fit

I'd be all wrinkles inside of it

And my baby brother's would be much too small

It just wouldn't cover me up at all

But I feel just right in the skin I wear

And there's nobody like me anywhere

– Anonymous

From: *Teacher Inservice Film/Inside/Out*